The Creative Curriculum® for Family Child Care, 2nd Edition

Volume 1: The Foundation

Diane Trister Dodge, Sherrie Rudick,
and Laura J. Colker

 **Teaching**Strategies™ • Washington D.C.

Editor: Laurie Taub
Design and layout: Abner Nieves
Illustrations: Anthony LeTourneau
Production: Judy Myers

Teaching Strategies, Inc.
P.O. Box 42243
Washington, DC 20015

www.TeachingStrategies.com
ISBN: Complete set: 978-1-60617-103-5
        Vol. 1: 978-1-60617-074-8
        Vol. 2: 978-1-60617-075-5

Teaching Strategies and The Creative Curriculum names and logos are registered trademarks of Teaching Strategies, Inc., Washington, D.C.

Library of Congress Cataloging-in-Publication Data

Dodge, Diane Trister.
    The creative curriculum for family child care / Diane Trister Dodge, Sherrie Rudick, and Laura J. Colker. -- 2nd ed.
        p. cm.
    Includes bibliographical references and index.
    ISBN 978-1-60617-074-8 (volume 1) -- ISBN 978-1-60617-075-5 (volume 2) 1. Family day care--Activity programs--United States. 2. Child development. I. Rudick, Sherrie. II. Colker, Laura J. (Laura Jean) III. Title.
    HV854.D63 2009
    362.7'12--dc22
                                                                                2009016355

Printed and bound in the United States of America

2014   2013   2012   2011   2010   2009   10 9 8 7 6 5 4 3 2 1

Acknowledgments

The first edition of *The Creative Curriculum for Family Child Care* was published in 1991. In the almost 20 years since that edition was written, the world of early childhood education, including family child care, changed greatly. We knew it was time to take on the challenging task of rewriting the curriculum entirely so that it reflects state-of-the-art knowledge of early childhood education in a family child care setting.

We began the process in 2004 by spending a day with M.-A. Lucas, Mary Ellen Pratt, Kathy Modigliani, and Martha Bozman, thinking expansively about family child care in the 21st century. They helped us develop a vision of what a revised curriculum should include.

When we had drafts of several chapters, Jeffrey Capizzano and Kelly Boyle, our Teaching Strategies research team, convened two focus groups of current family child care providers and family child care professional development experts. Focus group members encouraged us to strengthen our approach to the fact that many family child care providers care for children in groups of mixed ages. They also suggested that we offer more information about what and how children learn, and that we make *LearningGames* an integral part of the curriculum.

A thoughtful group of family child care experts reviewed the entire first draft of the manuscript. Thanks go to Julie Rae Gardner, Michelle Angry, Eva Hanshaw, Mary Margarita Contie, Lynda Addano Megan, Suzanne Williamson, Stacey Howe, Rosalyn Laney, and Nikki Darling-Kuria for affirming that we were moving in the right direction and for raising issues that needed to be rethought.

Special mention is due to three persons who guided us in innumerable ways. Debbie Enright answered countless questions about the life of a family child care provider and scrutinized every illustration with us. Donna Fowler and Amy Dapshanski made numerous suggestions for improving the manuscript; helped ensure that the curriculum supports NAFCC accreditation; and drafted "A Typical Day in Family Child Care," which is based on their many years of experience as family child care providers.

We owe much to Laurie Taub, our editor, whose content knowledge, sharp eyes, and graceful style ensured that the final product is engaging and our ideas clear. Laurie spent countless days and nights reading and rewriting, and her thoughtful and detailed editing shaped this book in more ways than we can describe.

Our illustrator, Anthony LeTourneau, created the beautiful illustrations that bring the children and family child care setting to life. We truly appreciated how patient and responsive he was to our many suggestions; he was committed to getting every picture right. Last but certainly not least, we thank Abner Nieves for the attractive and engaging design and layout of the book. Judy Myers handled production with marvelous energy, imagination, and patience.

Table of Contents

Volume 1

Part I: The Foundation

Introduction

Family child care is a growing profession. Today over a million family child care providers are caring for about 4 million children while their parents are at work.[1] As a member of this profession, you offer children and families a crucial service. You open your home, offering a safe environment where children feel comfortable and learn to build relationships with people other than the members of their immediate families. You work with children during the period of life when the greatest amount of development and learning occurs. You plan activities each day that support children's progress, helping them build a strong foundation for their success in school and in life. The partnerships you build with families and the knowledge that their children are in capable, loving hands enable them to attend to their work.

Many families choose family child care because they recognize and appreciate its important benefits. Family child care homes are often conveniently located in the communities where families live, and families are more likely to find providers who speak the families' home languages. Family child care providers often offer care for children of all ages and will accommodate siblings. Finding care for infants and toddlers is especially challenging, and families like the smaller, homey environment. Group sizes are small, so providers are able to give children more individual attention and maintain a calmer atmosphere. Perhaps the most important reason why families prefer family child care is that they can depend on reliable, loving, and responsive care from a knowledgeable person: you! You have chosen a very important profession.

What It Means to Be a Professional

A professional is a person who uses specialized knowledge and skills to do a job or provide a service. Child care is a profession that requires many different skills. In your work with children and families, you serve as an educator, a caregiver, a child development specialist, and often as a nutritionist and social worker. To care for children well, you must be knowledgeable about child development, how children learn, what children should be learning at each stage, and how to partner with families. Being a professional requires ongoing learning and a commitment to providing the very best service possible.

Most states have licensing requirements that apply to opening and operating a family child care program. The requirements vary considerably from state to state. These requirements usually address health and safety issues, but they rarely set standards for the educational program. Providers who view themselves as professionals, rather than as babysitters, are not content with simply meeting licensing requirements. They strive to achieve higher standards of quality. Those standards are set by the National Association for Family Child Care (NAFCC), a membership organization dedicated to promoting high-quality family child care by setting standards, supporting providers in meeting the standards through an accreditation process, and helping families understand the value of placing their children in an accredited family child care program. When you meet or exceed the standards set by your profession, you are a professional, someone who knows how to provide a high-quality program and who is therefore worthy of respect.

Many family child care providers join professional organizations such as NAFCC and the National Association for the Education of Young Children (NAEYC). Membership gives them access to the latest information about current issues in the field. Local child care resource and referral agencies offer community-based training and opportunities to network with other providers. Find out what providers are doing in your area and develop relationships with those who are also striving to achieve program excellence.

Why Quality Matters

High-quality care during the early years of life makes a profound and lasting difference. More brain development takes place in the first 3 years of life than during any other period. Every interaction and every bit of information a child receives by seeing, tasting, touching, smelling, and hearing affects the child's brain development. Furthermore, the trusting relationship you build with each child is central to healthy development and all learning.

High-quality care for preschool children prepares them to enter school ready to learn and succeed. A major study of child care programs by researchers at four universities found that children from all backgrounds who attended high-quality child care programs at ages 3 and 4 were better prepared for school than children in low-quality programs. They had stronger math, language, and social skills through second grade. The study also found that children who formed close relationships with their teachers had better social skills through elementary school. They had better thinking skills, were more able to attend to tasks, were more able to make friends, and had fewer behavioral problems.[2] Relationships matter, as do appropriate and engaging experiences in preschool.

The expectations for what preschool children should know and be able to do before entering kindergarten are more clearly defined today than in the past. Every state has developed, or is in the process of developing, early learning standards for 4-year-olds. Such standards provide guidance for planning learning experiences in early childhood programs. In addition to identifying knowledge and skills in content areas (literacy, mathematics, science, technology, social studies, and the arts), most state standards include objectives related to social–emotional skills, approaches to learning, and physical development. An increasing number of states are also developing standards for infants and toddlers. If you provide a prekindergarten program, it is important to become familiar with your state's early learning standards and to see how *The Creative Curriculum for Family Child Care* addresses those standards.

School-age children benefit from high-quality care as well. They need to be in safe places when they are not in school. They also need caring adults who provide structure and interesting activities. The family child care program should complement school and enable them to relax, socialize with peers and an adult, work on special projects, and become involved in the community beyond home and school.

Excellent care makes a difference for children of every age. The care children receive and their experiences in your program have a powerful influence on how they view the world, how they relate to others, and their ability to succeed as learners. Next to their families, you are probably the most important person in the lives of the children in your care. What you do every day is critical, so it cannot be left to chance. Providers who want to be thoughtful and intentional about the care they offer use a comprehensive curriculum and ongoing assessment to guide their work.

The Role of Curriculum in Family Child Care

A curriculum is like a road map because it helps you get where you want to go. A comprehensive, developmentally appropriate curriculum specifies objectives for children's development and learning. Objectives define what you want children to know and be able to do. The curriculum also tells you how to get there, how to help children achieve the objectives.

The Creative Curriculum for Family Child Care explains how to offer a high-quality program that meets the standards established by NAFCC. It also helps you address the early learning standards that most states have developed for children under age 5 and for children entering kindergarten. It describes the "what, why, how, when, and where" of providing care and education for children birth to age 12. It explains all aspects of a developmentally appropriate program and leads you through the processes of planning and implementing every aspect of caring for children and partnering with their families.

Just as a road map gives you choices about what routes to take, *The Creative Curriculum* offers choices and encourages flexibility. Caring for children is enjoyable and satisfying because of your ability to appreciate the everyday discoveries that delight a child: the bells that jingle in a pull toy, the amazing accomplishment of a first step, finally fitting a puzzle piece into place, learning to write, and finding the answers to interesting questions. *The Creative Curriculum* shows how everyday routines and experiences are opportunities to build relationships and promote learning. It helps you choose materials and plan experiences intentionally while still having flexibility to respond to the ever-changing interests and abilities of young children.

Family child care providers are educators as well as business owners. A curriculum addresses the first role, so you will find educational guidance in *The Creative Curriculum for Family Child Care.* Other resources are available to help you set up and manage the business aspects of caring for children in your home.

The Role of Curricular Objectives

The Creative Curriculum defines 36 objectives for the development and learning of all children (birth to age 6) and two more objectives for young dual-language learners. The objectives that relate to children's social–emotional, physical, oral language, and cognitive development are explained in chapter 1, "Knowing How Children Develop and Learn." The objectives for content learning—literacy, mathematics, science and technology, social studies, and the arts—are listed in chapter 3, "What Children Are Learning." A list of all 38 objectives is included in the appendix of this volume. (We do not define objectives for school-age children because they attend schools where their teachers use other curricula that specify learning objectives.)

Objectives serve several purposes. Because they define the development and learning you usually expect of children birth to age 6, they enable you to follow children's progress and celebrate their skills. By keeping the objectives in mind as you observe children every day, you find out what each child can do and what each child is ready to learn. Objectives also help you intentionally plan meaningful experiences for children of various ages. For example, when you involve children in making playdough, you can focus on the math skill of measuring ingredients, the literacy skill of following a picture recipe, and the motor skills used to mix and mold dough. Your emphasis might be different for each child, and your focus guides the way you interact with children during a particular experience. Throughout *The Creative Curriculum,* we show how one or more objectives can be addressed simultaneously through your interactions with children and the experiences you provide.

Fundamental Beliefs

A number of fundamental beliefs underlie *The Creative Curriculum for Family Child Care*. You probably already consider them central to your work.

- Responsive, individualized care is based on what you learn about each child.
- Ensuring children's safety and health is a critical program component.
- Care and learning environments must support and encourage play and exploration.
- Family child care providers and the children's families support children's development and learning by forming partnerships that respect cultural, family, and individual differences.
- Children's social–emotional development is a primary goal of the program.
- Dual-language learners must be supported as they learn more than one language.
- Children with disabilities must be included in all aspects of the program.

How the Curriculum Is Organized

The graphic on the right shows how the components of *The Creative Curriculum* fit together. Like the frame of a puzzle with many pieces, it offers a way to organize all aspects of the curriculum. *The Creative Curriculum* rests on a solid foundation of research and theory that are explained in the first section. Each of the 20 chapters also addresses a piece of the curriculum.

Here is an overview of what you will find:

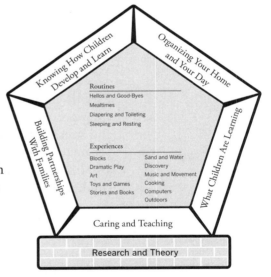

Volume 1 is "The Foundation." It begins with a section on the research and theory on which *The Creative Curriculum* is based, and it includes chapters 1–5.

> **The section "Applying Research and Theory to Practice"** explains the curriculum's focus on providing a safe and healthy environment, why relationships are the foundation for all learning, how children learn through play and interactions with people and their environment, the importance of individualizing learning, and why partnerships with families are essential. When you know the research and theory behind *The Creative Curriculum* approach, you can make and explain deliberate decisions about what you do.

> **Chapter 1, "Knowing How Children Develop and Learn,"** describes the social–emotional, physical, oral language, and cognitive development of infants, toddlers and twos, preschool children, and school-age children. It outlines the characteristics and experiences that make each child unique, including life circumstances, temperament, home languages, and disabilities.

Chapter 2, "Setting Up Your Home and Planning Your Day," offers guidance about organizing your space and materials and whether to use your entire home or part of it for child care. It shows how to create a daily schedule and make weekly plans in ways that give you direction but allow flexibility.

Chapter 3, "What Children Are Learning" shows how to foster learning through the positive relationship you form with each child, the interactions you have every day, and the materials and experiences you offer. What children should be learning and how they learn at each developmental stage are also discussed. That information is organized according to the content areas: language and literacy, mathematics, science, social studies, and the arts.

Chapter 4, "Caring and Teaching," offers strategies for building positive relationships, helping children develop self-regulation, and responding to challenging behaviors. It describes how to guide children's learning during daily routines and during experiences. Finally, it explains the role of ongoing assessment in learning about each child, following children's progress, and planning.

Chapter 5, "Building Partnerships With Families," explores the benefits of working with families as partners in the care of their children. It explains how partnerships are built from the first time you meet families and enroll their children. It discusses daily exchanges of information, communicating in respectful ways, and working through differences in ways that sustain the partnership and benefit the child.

Volume 2 has two parts.

Part II, "Routines," includes chapters 6–9. They discuss the four routines that make up an important part of the day: hellos and good-byes, mealtimes, diapering and toileting, and sleeping and resting. Each chapter begins by asking you to think about your personal views about the routine. The importance of each routine is explained, as well as setting up your home to make the day go smoothly. Guidance is given for involving children in routines and for partnering with families.

Part III, "Experiences," is comprised of chapters 10–20. They address the wide range of experiences you can offer children: blocks, dramatic play, art, toys and games, stories and books, sand and water, discovery, music and movement, cooking, computers, and outdoor play. Each chapter describes the selection and display of materials and ways to interact with children of different ages as they play with the materials you provide. Each also includes a letter to families explaining what children learn from the experience and what families can do at home.

LearningGames®

A set of 68 *LearningGames* activities is offered as part of *The Creative Curriculum for Family Child Care*. The activities are a resource to share with families and use in your own work with children. Four or five *LearningGames* activities are described at the end of each of the chapters on routines and experiences. In most, one activity is included for each age-group from birth to age 5. Ways to share them with families are also suggested. Each *LearningGames* activity shows how everyday interactions and games that adults play with children lead to positive relationships and important learning. Each game sheet includes information about what the child is experiencing, how she or he may react to the game, and an explanation of why the activity is important for the child's development. Each game is illustrated, includes clear directions, offers ideas for extending the activity, and lists a children's book that is related to the game. A chart in the appendix of volume 2 identifies which curricular objectives are addressed through each activity.

The 68 activities were selected from a set of 200 *LearningGames* that have been validated by 21 years of research showing positive gains for children that last through the school-age period and into early adulthood.[3] Careful research conducted in eight states found that children who participate in many of these games in child care and at home have better measured development than those who do not play them or who play only a few.[4] Because of the research findings, we have made them an important part of *The Creative Curriculum for Family Child Care.* Many of the teaching strategies we describe in chapter 4, "Caring and Teaching," are used in these *LearningGames* activities. These are the strategies: acknowledging and describing, coaching, extending, demonstrating, and giving information. By using the activities and sharing them with families, you contribute to a true partnership for supporting their children's learning at home and in your program.

Imagining a Typical Day

If you are just starting a program, you may be wondering what is involved in caring for a group of children of different ages in your home. If you are experienced, you may be curious about how your program compares with others. To give you an idea of what an ordinary day might be like, we invite you to find a comfortable chair and read the following story, "A Typical Day in Family Child Care." As you will see, we have imagined a group of seven children who appear in this story and throughout the chapters on routines and experiences. They are formally "introduced" in chapter 1. We invite you to place yourself in the role of the provider because *The Creative Curriculum* is addressed to you.

A Typical Day in Family Child Care

Preparation and Family Responsibilities

Well before the children arrive, you begin to prepare for the day. First you make a quart of fresh bleach solution so that you'll be ready to clean toys and surfaces throughout the day. Then you check the paint supplies to make sure the children will have enough. Remembering that Nathan was very excited yesterday about the train ride he took last weekend with his parents, you decide to build on this new interest. In the closet, you find a train set and books about trains. The children have not seen them before, so you set them on a table. You look up the Spanish word for *train* so you can use it as you introduce the materials to Jorge and Rosa. Then you look at your menu and begin to prepare breakfast for the children. You make one last check before their arrival, glancing in the bathroom to be sure that soap, paper towels, toilet paper, and a step stool are in place. Then you wake your daughter, Keisha (4 1/2 years), point out two outfits, and ask her to choose one. You accompany her to the bathroom and talk with her as she brushes her teeth, washes her hands and face, and gets dressed. While brushing her hair, you ask Keisha if she wants to have breakfast right away or wait until some of her friends arrive. She decides to wait. When you both go to the living room, Keisha takes out the collage materials and continues to work on a project she started several days ago.

Arrival

Tamika (19 months) and Tyrone (8 years) arrive first. You greet each child and their mother by name, offer a big smile, hug the children, and ask their mother how the evening went yesterday. As you converse, you check quickly to be sure that the children do not seem sick, as you check every arriving child. When their mother leaves, Tyrone, Tamika, and you wave good-bye to her. You ask Tyrone if he is ready for school and invite him and Tamika to look at books or play with puzzles. Noticing that Tyrone is eyeing the train on the table, you show the train set to them and talk about train travel. Both children are interested in the set, and Tyrone enthusiastically helps Tamika connect the pieces of track. When the track is finished, Tyrone loses interest and asks whether he may use the computer. You help him get started on the computer while Tamika starts exploring the train cars and Keisha continues pasting her collage.

Jeremy (8 months) is next to arrive. You greet him and his mother warmly. You talk with Jeremy's mother about his schedule at home and how he ate and slept. Jeremy's mother hands you an insulated bag that contains several bottles of breast milk that she expressed. She tells you that the milk is fresh and the bottles are dated. She explains that Jeremy is getting hungry but she is running too late to feed him as she does most mornings when they arrive. She asks you to feed him as soon as possible. After you thank her for the bottles and information, you and Jeremy say good-bye. As his mother walks away, Jeremy begins to cry. You give him a hug and say, "I know you'll miss your mommy. She'll be back later to pick you up. Are you hungry? Let's go warm your bottle." You carry Jeremy to the kitchen, where you place one of the bottles in a container of hot water and put the remaining bottles in the refrigerator. Jeremy nestles into your arms.

When the milk is warm, you sit down at the table next to Tamika, who is still playing with the train. You hold Jeremy in your arms, positioning him so that you can make eye contact with him while he drinks. Keisha brings her collage over to show you and then asks you to hold her. You hug her, saying, "Okay, my little sunshine. I will hold you as soon as Jeremy finishes his bottle. In the meantime, will you please put the collage materials away and wash your hands? Let's also find a good place to hang your collage. I'm glad that you signed your artwork."

Rosa (4 years) and Nathan (3 years) arrive next. You hold Jeremy as you greet their families. Rosa reaches up to pat Jeremy. You smile at Rosa and say, "¡Buenos dias, Rosa! Como esta"?

Rosa replies, "Bien".

You say, "I'm glad you're well today!" Then you turn to Nathan. "Good morning, Nathan. How are you today?"

Nathan replies, "¡Bien"!

This delights you because you know that Nathan has trouble speaking and *bien* is a new word for him. You say, "Nathan, you are learning Spanish by talking with Rosa! I'm glad you're feeling well, too." You remind Nathan's father that the children are finishing their study of trees, and you ask him if he will be able to participate in the final celebration next Friday. Rosa's mother tells you she will be picking Rosa up early that afternoon for a doctor's appointment, so neither she nor Rosa will be able to be part of the celebration. You ask her and Nathan's father about alternative dates and say you'll let them know which day will be best for most of the families.

Breakfast

Tamika interrupts you, tugging on your pants and insisting, "Eat, eat!" Jeremy squirms to get down, so you place him on the living room rug where you can still see him from the kitchen. He pulls some of his favorite toys off the low shelf and begins to play with them. You turn to Keisha, Tamika, and Tyrone and say, "Let's clean up and get ready for breakfast. Let's wash our hands so we can eat." You help Tamika turn on the water and wash her hands, singing, "This Is the Way We Wash Our Hands," and you use a paper towel to turn off the water together when finished. Then you wash your own hands, and the other children wash and dry theirs.

Tyrone passes out the plates while Nathan puts out the napkins and Rosa places the silverware. Meanwhile, you put Tamika in her high chair. You pick Jeremy up, wash his hands, and then place him in another high chair. You pull the two high chairs up to the table and place the food on the table so the children can help themselves, family style. As the children pass the food to each other, you encourage the older children to serve themselves. You ask Nathan what he is eating. As he points, you say, "You have toast today," and wait for him to repeat the word *toast*. You place a sippy cup of water, a few Cheerios®, and some banana slices on Jeremy's tray, and he immediately puts a piece of cereal in his mouth. You sit near the high chairs so that you can talk and eat with the children and assist Tamika and Jeremy if they need help. You talk about plans for the day, noting to yourself that none of the parents alerted you to anything that might affect the children's day.

After breakfast, the older children put their plates and cups on the counter. You check Tamika's and Jeremy's diapers and find that both need to be changed. After changing Jeremy's diaper, washing Jeremy's hands, and sanitizing the changing surface, you wash your hands before changing Tamika. Meanwhile, the other children use the bathroom and wash their hands. Then you help Tamika wash her hands and remind Tyrone to get ready to leave for school. You and the children walk Tyrone to the bus stop as you talk with them about safety rules. The children and you tell Tyrone good-bye as he boards the bus.

Outdoor Time

It's a beautiful day, so you decide to change the schedule and play outdoors before doing anything else. Pointing out the large appliance boxes that the children have been playing with for several days, you suggest that they make a train out of the boxes and pretend they are taking a ride like the one Nathan's family took last weekend. Jorge (2 1/2 years) arrives as the children are arranging the boxes, and he runs to see what they are doing. You greet Jorge's mother and comment on Jorge's enthusiasm. Jorge's mother smiles, calls good-bye to Jorge, and leaves. You say, "Buenos dias, Jorge. Welcome aboard our train." Then you get a prop box of costumes from the shed for the children to use as they play.

Nathan says, "D'ive" and pretends to steer.

Keisha says, "Okay, Nathan, here's your hat. I'm going to be in the caboose."

"Mí, también", Jorge chimes in.

Rosa decides she wants to play with balls. You suggest that she and Tamika roll balls back and forth, and you kick a ball to Rosa lightly. Jeremy points at a bird flying overhead, and you say, "Yes, you see a crow," imitating a crow caw for Jeremy. When it is about time to go in, you tell the children that they have 5 more minutes to play. You notice that Jeremy is rubbing his eyes.

Morning Circle, Read-Aloud, and Snack

The children troop inside. You check Jeremy's and Tamika's diapers and find that only Jeremy's needs changing. After changing his diaper and washing both your hands and Jeremy's, you lay him down for a nap, placing him on his back in his crib. You help the children wash their hands and ask them to sit down for circle time. You begin with a morning song and then do a fingerplay. You go over the safety rules they have been talking about and then prompt a conversation about the train they constructed with the boxes. Next you pick up a new book, *Chugga-Chugga Choo-Choo*, by Kevin Lewis, to read to them. The children are excited to learn that the book is about an imaginary train like the one they just made. The book is filled with rhymes and predictable phrases that the children love saying with you, like "Chugga-chugga choo-choo, whistle blowing, whooooooooo! Whooooooooo!" You notice that Nathan is able to say "Whooooooooo!" clearly.

After a while, both Tamika and Jorge leave the circle to play with toys. They glance at you occasionally as you read with Nathan, Rosa, and Keisha. Jorge decides to return to the circle to listen to the train book. Tamika listens from a distance. Every time you get to the refrain, Jorge shouts, "Chugga-chugga choo-choo, whistle blowing, whooooooooo! Whooooooooo!" You smile and hug him.

A little later, Jeremy is still sleeping, and Jorge and Nathan are playing with the train. Keisha is sitting at the dining room table, rolling some playdough, while Rosa sits opposite her, drawing. You take Tamika by the hand and ask her to help you set food on the table so the children can help themselves to a morning snack. As you place word and picture signs that invite the children to take four crackers and four apple slices, you explain to Tamika what you are doing. You then tell all of the children that the snack is ready for them to get when they are hungry. You review the sign cards with them and remind them to wash their hands before they take their snack and after they finish eating. As Keisha gets her snack, you hear her say, "These crackers are squares."

You agree, "Yes, they are. How did you know that?"

Keisha responds, "'Cause they have four sides, and all the sides are the same." You ask, "Are all crackers square?" Keisha laughs, "No, some are circles, and some are fish!" As the children finish their snack, they throw their napkins away and place their cups on the counter. When all the children have had a snack, Nathan washes the snack table.

Morning Choice Time

You tell the children, "Today you may choose to paint, play with playdough or clay, draw, build with blocks, play with the train set or other toys, dress up and pretend, work at the computer, look at books, listen to music, or write. Think about what you want to do." Keisha and Rosa head toward the dramatic play area. Jorge begins painting while Nathan looks to you for guidance. You show Nathan pictures of the various choices and name each one with him. He points to the picture of the train, and you prompt, "You want to play with the train today."

Nathan smiles and says, "Train. Now."

As you change Tamika's diaper, you ask her where she would like to play. She points to Nathan. "Let's wash our hands. Then you may join Nathan." Meanwhile, Jeremy begins to whimper. You pick him up saying, "Did you have a good nap, Mr. Jeremy? We're glad you are awake now. Let's change that diaper so you are more comfortable."

After laying him gently on the changing table, you change his diaper and talk to him about his toes, which he grabs and releases with great delight. After cleaning and sanitizing the changing table and washing hands, you take him to the kitchen, place him in a high chair, and say, "I'm going to get your lunch ready now. I know you are hungry. Here is a cracker for you to eat while you wait. I'll put some fresh water in your sippy cup, too." After checking to see that the other children are happily engaged, you sit down and begin feeding Jeremy. Between spoonfuls of pureed carrots, Jeremy waves another spoon and takes a few sips from his cup. You take a bottle of his mother's expressed milk out of the refrigerator and begin warming it in a container of hot water. You pick Jeremy up from the high chair, wash his face, help him wash his hands, and then wash your own. You take Jeremy back to the kitchen, get his bottle, and then sit on the floor next to Nathan and Tamika, holding Jeremy in your arms. You sing to Jeremy softly as he drinks his bottle and watches Nathan and Tamika play with the train. When Jeremy finishes his bottle, you place him on a blanket with a couple of his favorite toys. He especially enjoys toys he can hold and bang together.

Keisha and Rosa approach you, offering plates of make-believe food. You pretend to eat the food saying, "Mmm, this is delicious. How did you make this delicious snack?" Then you ask the girls if they will write a menu for today's lunch. As the girls scurry to the writing table to make a menu, Jorge brings his picture to show you. You describe it, saying, "I see you used a lot of bright colors: red, purple, and yellow. Tell me about your painting."

Jorge tells you that it is a train that goes "Chugga-chugga choo-choo." You laugh together and ask Jorge how he would say that in Spanish. Jorge thinks for a moment and says, "Chugga-chugga choo-choo!" Laughing together, you invite Jorge to show Nathan and Tamika his painting. After the children admire Jorge's painting, you ask him to help you find a place on the refrigerator to display it. Afterwards, you sit with Jeremy on your lap, talking with Nathan, Tamika, and Jorge about what they are doing as they play with the train.

Things are going well until Jorge pulls a train car out of Tamika's hand. Tamika starts to cry, and Jorge buries the car in his lap. After talking to Jorge about the importance of being kind, you hand Tamika a similar train car. You know that providing duplicates helps children avoid frustration until they are ready to learn to share.

When Nathan lines the train cars up according to a pattern of red, blue, green; red, blue, green; etc. You comment about that. You review the pattern out loud, pointing to a corresponding car as you say the name of each color. You ask the children to repeat each color name after you say it, and you wait long enough for Tamika and Nathan to say it, too. Then you lead the children in laying out the next three colors in Nathan's pattern. Delighted, you take a photo of the children as they continue the pattern with the cars.

Lunch

As choice time near ends, you give the children a 5-minute warning, telling them that it will soon be time to clean up the toys and get ready for lunch. You check Tamika's diaper as the children wash their hands. Then you help Tamika wash her hands and wash your own.

In the kitchen, you set Jeremy down on a blanket with some vinyl books to explore for a few minutes. You take out the sandwiches and salad that you prepared the previous evening and place them on the table. The older children set the table. You put Tamika in her high chair and serve her. The older children sit down and pass the plate of halved sandwiches and the bowl of salad. They serve themselves, family style. You pick Jeremy up and sit at the table with him in your lap. He has already eaten, but you want him to be part of the social experience. You pull Tamika's high chair close to the table, making a cozy grouping. As you and the children eat, you lead them in a lively discussion of the morning's events. Jeremy waves a small piece of bread enthusiastically. As they finish, the older children scrape their plates, put them on the counter, use the bathroom, wash their hands, brush their teeth, and prepare to nap. You put Jeremy down where you can see him while you help Tamika brush her teeth. Then you change her diaper, help her wash her hands, and wash your own hands.

Read-Aloud and Rest Time

After the cots are set up, you gather the children to read a story aloud. At Jorge's suggestion, you read *Dinosaur VS. Bedtime*, by Lane Shea. Jorge has requested this book all week. He loves the idea that the dinosaur has trouble staying awake, just as he does. As you are reading, Tamika starts nodding off, and you suggest that she listen to the rest of the story from her cot. When the story ends, Nathan, Rosa, and Keisha lie down on their cots. Holding Jeremy, you cover the children, pat each one, and tell them you will see them when they wake up. "Sleep tight," you say as you take Jeremy to the kitchen so you can clean up from lunch. Keisha plays quietly on her cot with her doll as the others fall asleep.

While you clean up the kitchen, Jeremy has tummy time on a blanket where you can watch each other. When you are done cleaning, you sit down to play peek-a-boo and other interactive games with him. Jeremy giggles but soon starts to rub his eyes. You say, "It looks like you're getting sleepy, too, Jeremy." You change his diaper again, wash his hands and your own, and lay him on his back in his crib.

While the children are resting, you date the train photo, write a short description of what the children were doing when you took it, and add it to Nathan's portfolio. Now you have a little time to sit down and think about the day. Clearly, a number of the children are very interested in trains. Maybe this is a good time to plan a trip to the local train station with the children. You look up some fingerplays and songs about trains so you can teach them to the children. You wonder if the children are interested enough in trains for that to be a good topic for a study. You decide to explore this idea at your morning meeting tomorrow. After jotting some notes to yourself, you check to be sure the children are resting well. Then you go over some paperwork and write a shopping list. You think about the novel you started to read last week and wonder whether you have time to read a little before the children wake up. Doubting that possibility, you pour some tea and enjoy a few minutes of quiet before setting out the children's afternoon snack.

Afternoon Experiences

As the children begin to wake up, you give them each a hug and have them use the bathroom and comb their hair. Each child picks something quiet to play with until everyone is awake. Those who are hungry help themselves to orange sections, whole wheat crackers, and water that you put out for them on the table. Tamika and Jeremy wake up last. You hug them, change their diapers, and wash their hands and yours. You put some simple puzzles on a blanket for the babies, but Tamika wants to join the older girls, who are working with playdough at the table.

At three o'clock, everyone prepares to walk to the bus stop to meet Tyrone. During the walk, the children count the cars and buses that pass. When Tyrone steps off the school bus, the children give him a hug. You talk to Tyrone about his day and his plans for the afternoon. Arriving back home, Tyrone talks with the children as he takes yogurt and a granola muffin out of the refrigerator for his snack. The children tell Tyrone excitedly about their box train in the backyard. After a while, Tyrone sits down to do his homework while the other children choose from the activities that you suggest: drawing, playdough, trains, puzzles, blocks, computer, discovery, and books. Keisha and Rosa sit down at the discovery table and take out the rock collection. They begin weighing the rocks on the balance scale and "writing" the weights in a journal. Jorge and Nathan play with the LEGOS® while you sit on the floor and read a book to Tamika and Jeremy. When Tyrone is finished with his assignments, you ask him if he'd like to play outside with the other children. When he says, "Yes," you ask him to carry some paper, crayons, and markers outside in case anyone wants to draw or write at the picnic table.

Outside Time and Departure

The children eagerly run outside to play, pulling Tyrone along with them to show him their box train. Tyrone announces that he will be the engineer. Rosa and Keisha decide to be passengers. They tell Nathan that he may be the conductor. Nathan yells, "All 'board!" and begins to collect pretend tickets. Tamika and Jeremy peek into the boxes, laughing.

Rosa's mother comes to take her home. You chat briefly about Rosa's day and remind her please to get a copy of Rosa's immunization record while they are at the doctor's office. Keisha gives Rosa a hug.

Jeremy's mother arrives next. When he sees her, Jeremy squeals and holds his arms toward her. His mother picks him up and gives him a big kiss. You tell her about Jeremy's naps, what he ate, and what else he did during the day. When his mother prompts him, Jeremy waves good-bye as they leave.

When Jorge's father arrives and joins him near the box train, Jorge tells him about it excitedly. You explain how much Jorge seems to like trains and that you would like to take the children to the local train station. Jorge leaves with his father, talking about trains in Spanish. You listen, hoping to pick up some Spanish vocabulary.

Nathan's mother comes next. You talk to her about Nathan's continued interest in trains and the possibility of doing a study about trains. Excited, you tell her about the color pattern he made with the train cars. You both share the joy of this major accomplishment. When he can hear you, you do not talk about what Nathan cannot yet do, and you know that Nathan's mother gets discouraged when people focus primarily on his needs. You do tell her how helpful it has been to work with Nathan's speech therapist and how all of the children are benefitting from the strategies she has taught you for supporting Nathan. Nathan gives you a good-bye hug.

When Tamika's and Tyrone's father arrives, you tell him about the homework Tyrone completed and how eager the younger children were to share their train with him. You report that Tamika also enjoyed playing with the new train set and squishing playdough with the older girls. Tamika and Tyrone both give you good-bye hugs.

You take Keisha's hand, saying, "Now it's just the two of us for a little while. Come; sit on my lap. Let's talk about the day. Then you can help me straighten up a bit. I have a new song I want to sing with you if you'd like to learn it."

Getting Started

Has reading "A Typical Day in Family Child Care" given you an idea of what it is like to care for children of different ages in your home? If you have been operating a program for some time, does the story sound familiar? Whether you are a new or an experienced provider, we hope the story energizes you for your very important work.

The Creative Curriculum for Family Child Care is a comprehensive resource for planning and implementing your program. It covers all aspects of providing care and education for children and offers a range of choices. It may seem like a lot of information. Do not feel as though you have to read the entire book at once. Find the topics that are of most importance to your work and start with those chapters. If you are just setting up your program, you may be seeking guidance about organizing your home and planning your day (chapter 2). Perhaps you want ideas about welcoming families and enrolling children (chapter 5). If you have been operating a program for a while, pick a routine that presents some challenges and try the suggestions in that chapter. Choose one of the experiences that particularly interests you and try some new ideas. Become familiar with the objectives for children's development and learning by posting them as a reminder of where you are heading. Remember, *The Creative Curriculum* is your road map for getting there. We hope you enjoy the journey!

[1] National Association for Family Child Care. (2006). *Provider's self-study workbook: Quality standards for NAFCC accreditation.* Salt Lake City, UT: NAFCC.

[2] Peisner-Feinberg, E. S., Burchinal, M. R., Clifford, R. M., Culkin, M. L., Howes, C., Kagan, S. L., et al. (2000). *The children of the cost, quality, and outcomes study go to school: Technical report.* Chapel Hill: University of North Carolina at Chapel Hill, Frank Porter Graham Child Development Center.

[3] Campbell, F. A., Ramey, C. T., Pungello, E., Sparling, J., & Miller-Johnson, S. (2002). Early childhood education: Young adult outcomes from the Abecedarian Project. *Applied Developmental Science, 6*(1), 42–57.

[4] Sparling, J., Lewis, I., Ramey, C. T., Wasik, B. H., Bryant, D. M., LaVange, L. M. (1991). Partners: A curriculum to help premature, low-birth-weight infants get off to a good start. *Topics in Early Childhood Special Education, 11*(1), 36–55.

Applying Research and Theory to Practice

Applying Research and Theory to Practice

Having a high-quality family child care program means that you act in the ways that are best for children. To do that, you must understand why particular strategies and approaches are considered best practices and why the curricular objectives are important. We turn to research findings to understand how children develop and learn.

This section explains the major research and theory that guide *The Creative Curriculum for Family Child Care.* When you are familiar with this research, you will know why it is important to respond quickly to a crying baby and talk with children during routines and experiences. You will also understand why play is absolutely necessary even though you might feel pressured to focus on academics. You can be confident that your program is based on a solid foundation.

This chapter explores four guiding principles on which *The Creative Curriculum for Family Child Care* is based. They guide practice and help us understand the reasons for intentionally setting up and carrying out family child care programs in particular ways. These are the principles:

- Relationships are the foundation for learning.
- Children learn through play.
- Children learn by interacting with people and their environments.
- Partnerships with families are essential.

Relationships: The Foundation for Learning

Nurturing, stable relationships with adults are central to every child's development. **Attachment theory** describes the process by which babies bond with the important people in their lives. Children who develop secure attachments to one or more adults are more likely to develop positive social skills and to be emotionally secure.[1] Moreover, children who have secure attachments are more curious and perform better in school than children with less secure attachments.[2] Secure attachments develop when adults consistently, appropriately, and lovingly care for infants and meet their basic needs (i.e., to be fed, changed, given rest, kept safe, stimulated, and comforted). Consistent, nurturing care teaches children that they are important and helps them develop a positive sense of self.

Famous psychologist **Erik Erikson**[3] theorized that the child's first psychological task is to develop trust. Babies who receive consistent and loving care learn to trust others, themselves, and the world around them. When they feel safe, babies feel free to explore. Children learn about their world within the security of trusting relationships with caregivers. As they explore and experiment, children gain knowledge. Erikson also thought it is important for children to develop autonomy and initiative. Those terms refer to doing things independently, developing confidence in one's own abilities, taking on new tasks, and completing them.

Child psychiatrist and psychoanalyst **Stanley Greenspan**[4] views the infant's development of trusting relationships as a milestone in his or her emotional growth. By 5 months of age, some infants eagerly seek social interaction. They return your smiles, watch your face with great interest, and relax when held. Others are more hesitant. These infants need you and their parents to continue to reach out to them, even when they ignore or reject some of your attempts to engage them. All children need to develop secure attachments. Mastery of this milestone means that a baby has learned that relationships can be joyful and that warmth and love are possible.

We now know that relationships do not just provide a context for learning, they actually affect the way the brain develops.[5] The absence of warm, secure relationships can be devastating to children.[6] Nurturing and positive interactions release chemicals that promote brain development. Without the support and comfort of a close personal relationship, children cannot cope with stress.

What This Means for Your Practice

Provide responsive, loving care. Keep each child safe and healthy, offer comfort and affection, and share the joy of everyday experiences by interacting with each child.

Use routines, such as hellos and good-byes, diapering and toileting, mealtimes, and sleeping and resting, to develop a trusting relationship with each child.

Talk to all children one-on-one as well as in groups. Let children know that you care about what they think and how they feel. Give children nonverbal cues to tell them that they are valued. Reach out to every child, including those who are hesitant.

Use relationships to guide children's learning and encourage their continuing efforts. Instead of expecting children always to follow an adult's lead, often let them initiate activities among themselves and with you.

Comfort and otherwise respond intentionally to children, especially those who are under stress.

Learning Through Play

Children learn about themselves, other people, and the world by playing. Play takes many forms. For example, a baby drops a wooden bead into a container again and again, a toddler bangs the keys of a piano, a preschooler sinks objects in a tub of water, and a school-age child flies a kite. As they play, children acquire language, learn to solve problems, learn to control their behavior and feelings, and explore social roles.

One of the first persons to recognize the importance of play was **Jean Piaget,**[7] a Swiss philosopher, scientist, and developmental theorist. According to Piaget, play serves many purposes and provides an excellent vehicle for learning. By handling many different materials, children learn to observe, compare, sort, and sequence them. Their knowledge grows as they experiment, make discoveries, and modify their current thinking to incorporate new insights.

Building on Piaget's theory about how play helps children learn, Russian psychologist **Lev Vygotsky**[8] argued that children think in complex ways as they play. They make rules, use symbols, and create narratives. Vygotsky thought that adults and competent peers enhance a child's ability to learn through play. He used the term *zone of proximal development* (ZPD) to explain how learning takes place during play. The lower limit of the zone is what a child can learn by playing independently. The upper limit of the zone is what a child can learn by watching and talking to peers and adults. With the guidance and support of a teacher or provider, children build new knowledge by fitting new information and experiences with what they already know. Vygotsky found that in sociodramatic play, which is characterized by high levels of pretending, children to talk to themselves and each other about what they are playing and how they are going to play. He thought that such talk enhances self-regulation, the ability to control one's emotions and behavior and to resist impulses. More recent research has confirmed the validity of Vygotsky's theories. **Laura Berk's** studies of children's play explored the relationship between pretend play and self-regulation.[9] Similarly, play researcher **Sara Smilansky** found that children who engaged in high levels of sociodramatic play in preschool performed better academically in fourth grade than peers whose preschool play was less mature.[10] The research findings are strong: Pretend play is related strongly to self-regulation and academic achievement.

What This Means for Your Practice

Provide all children with opportunities to play, including school-age children. Children of all ages need to play.

Provide at least an hour of free, unstructured play daily so children have opportunities to make choices and decisions, solve problems, pursue their interests, build language and literacy skills, discover mathematical relationships, be scientists, and see themselves as competent.

Observe children's interests and build on them. Ask probing questions that will stretch children's thinking: "How else might you…?" "In what ways is this similar to…?" "How can you solve that problem?" Play with children one-on-one and encourage small-group work with peers.

Encourage children to engage in make-believe play with at least two other children. Invite children to make up scenarios. Encourage children to remind themselves and each other of what they decided to do and say as they play.

Provide long periods of unstructured, imaginative play. Realistic props are good for very young children, but encourage preschoolers and older children to use more abstract props.

Learning by Interacting With People and the Environment

Piaget found that children learn through the direct manipulation of objects and by using all of their senses. As described by Piaget, learning is a dynamic process with a number of stages. He explained that children must engage in tasks actively in order to develop and learn. Children seek and process new information on the basis of what they already know. They also modify their thinking in order to make sense of new information and experiences.

Vygotsky found that children need to be able to talk about problems in order to solve them and talk about concepts in order to understand and apply them. In his theory, thought and language are intertwined. As a child discusses a problem or task with an adult, the adult supplies language to assist the child in solving or doing it. The child gradually internalizes the language and more mature thought processes. Eventually, responsibility for the task is shifted from the adult to the child. The instructional technique in which an adult helps the child gradually develop higher level skills has become known as *scaffolding*.

Over the past 20 years, scientists have been able to study neurological aspects of how children learn. We call their work **brain research**. Studies have confirmed that a safe and predictable physical environment and the quality and continuity of day-to-day care contribute significantly to healthy brain development and learning.[11]

Brain research also shows that children's cognitive, emotional, and social capabilities are intertwined. Academic learning cannot be separated from social–emotional growth. Children's physical and emotional well-being are closely linked to their ability to think and learn effectively. For children to excel in school, educators need to address all aspects of their development.

We have also learned more about how the brain functions. Early experiences and interactions directly affect the physical structure of the brain. For a brain connection to become permanent, it must be used repeatedly. Connections that are not used eventually disappear.

Brain research has shown us that, even though the brain continues to change in response to experiences throughout life, there are sensitive periods for certain kinds of learning (including emotional control, social attachment, and language). These are times when children are most receptive to what the environment has to offer. Most of these optimal times for learning are during the early childhood years. However, questions about the brain areas involved in various kinds of learning are still being explored. Although particular kinds of learning are easier at certain times, learning continues throughout life unless circumstances are extreme. It appears as though the brain remains open, so appropriate experiences are important.

What This Means for Your Practice

Teach the whole child. Remember that social–emotional, physical, cognitive, and language development are intertwined.

Give children many choices and chances to investigate how things work. Allow children time to explore and experiment with books, art materials, music, dramatic play, sand and water, blocks, toys and games, cooking, computers, and the outdoors.

Encourage children to solve problems and take appropriate risks.

Model self-talk that supports children's cognitive development (thinking). Offer ideas about how to approach tasks.

Surround children with language. Sing and read with them and have back-and-forth vocal exchanges with them even before children can speak. If you have dual-language learners, support them as they learn more than one language.

Offer opportunities for children to work together.

Essential Partnerships With Families

When children receive consistent messages and support from both their families and their care providers, everyone benefits. Family participation involves both formal and informal connections between parents and their children's educational programs. Your regular communication with the children's families is critical to the children's development and learning.

Four decades of research confirm the importance of strong partnerships between families and early childhood programs. Bonds between homes and programs enhance children's problem-solving skills and social competency, and they can reduce aggression at home and at the educational program.[12] Indeed, a successful home–program relationship can help overcome the effects of poverty. Moreover, these benefits are sustained over time.[13]

Research also underscores the need to reach out to fathers and other extended family members. Paternal participation is linked with both school readiness and children's emotional self-regulation.[14]

What This Means for Your Practice

Develop positive relationships with families, both formally and informally.

Communicate with families regularly. Hold family conferences, share information in person and by phone, and send newsletters and e-mail messages.

Encourage children's families to volunteer in your program. Invite them to join field trips and eat meals with the children.

Reach out to all family members. Everyone who is special to a young child has an important role.

Summary

Our understanding of best practice in early childhood education is shaped by the researchers and theorists who laid the groundwork for our thinking about how children develop and learn. Their work is the foundation for defining high-quality early childhood education and care.

The research described in this chapter validates and expands our knowledge. As a family child care provider, you translate research and theory into practice every day. The ways you set up your program, plan your day, interact with children and families, and follow learning objectives for children are informed by this research. Being familiar with the research makes you a knowledgeable professional.

[1] Siegel, D. J. (1999). *The developing mind: Toward a science of neurobiology of interpersonal experience.* New York: Guilford Press.

[2] Wiggins, P. (2000). Infant brain development: Making the research work for early childhood programs. *Texas Child Care Quarterly, 23*(4), 2–8.

[3] Erikson, E. H. (1950). *Childhood and society.* New York: Norton.

[4] Greenspan, S. I. (with Greenspan, N. T.). (1985). *First feelings: Milestones in the emotional development of your infant and child from birth to age 4.* New York: Viking Press.

[5] Shore, R. (1997). *Rethinking the brain: New insights into early development.* New York, NY: Families and Work Institute.

[6] National Scientific Council on the Developing Child. (2004). *Young children develop in an environment of relationships* (Working paper no. 1). Cambridge, MA: Author.

[7] Piaget, J. (1972). *Play, dreams, and imitation in childhood.* London: Routledge and Kegan Paul. (Original work published in 1945)

[8] Vygotsky, L. S. (1978). *Mind in society: The development of higher psychological processes.* Cambridge, MA: Harvard University Press. (Original work published in 1934)

[9] Elias, C. L., & Berk, L. E. (2002). Self-regulation in young children: Is there a role for sociodramatic play? *Early Childhood Research Quarterly, 17*(1), 6–238.

[10] Smilansky, S., & Shefatya, L. (1990). *Facilitating play: A medium for promoting cognitive, socio-emotional and academic development in young children.* Gaithersburg, MD: Psychosocial and Educational Publications.

[11] Shonkoff, J. P., & Phillips, D. A. (Eds.). (2000). *From neurons to neighborhoods: The science of early childhood development.* Washington, DC: National Academies Press.

National Association of Social Workers. (2008). *Early childhood development current trends.* Retrieved October 22, 2008, from http://wwww.helpstartshere.org/Default.aspx?PageID=383

National Scientific Council on the Developing Child. (2004). *Young children develop in an environment of relationships* (Working paper no. 1). Cambridge, MA: Author.

Oberklaid, F. (2006). *Early brain development: Implications for work with young children and their families.* Melbourne, Australia: Centre for Community Child Health.

[12] Ou, S. (2005). Pathways of long-term effects of an early intervention program on educational attainment: Findings from the Chicago longitudinal study. *Applied Developmental Psychology, 37*(4), 379–402.

[13] Harvard Family Research Project. (Spring 2006). *Family involvement in early childhood education* (No. 1). Retrieved October 22, 2008, from http://www.hfrp.org/publications-resources/browse-our-publications/family-involvement-in-early-childhood-education

[14] Downer, J. T., & Mendez, J. L. (2005). African American father involvement and preschool children's school readiness. *Early Education and Development, 16*(3), 317–40.

Knowing How Children Develop and Learn

Knowing How Children Develop and Learn

The Creative Curriculum for Family Child Care is based on research and theory about child development. This enables you to build a program that meets the needs, interests, and abilities of all the children in your care, no matter what their ages. When you know what to expect of children at each stage of development, you can create a responsive environment and plan appropriate experiences for the children in your family child care program. Being responsive to children's developmental strengths and needs is the best way to support their development and learning.

In addition to knowing how children typically develop and learn, it is also important to recognize that children develop at their own rates and learn in their own ways. This chapter will provide you with information you need to meet children's developmental and individual needs. It highlights some of the ways you can create a responsive program.

This chapter includes three sections:

What Children Are Generally Like shows you how to use your knowledge of typical child development. Four areas of development are discussed: social–emotional, cognitive, language, and physical. In this section, we also introduce you to the children who are cared for in our example of *The Creative Curriculum* family child care home—yours!

Objectives for Development and Learning: Birth to Age 6 presents 14 objectives for social–emotional development, physical development, oral language development, and cognitive development. (Twenty-four additional objectives for content area learning are addressed in chapter 3, "What Children Are Learning.")

Individual Differences discusses the ways in which life circumstances, temperament, home language, and a disability may affect the individual development of children.

What Children Are Generally Like

Your knowledge of typical child development is the starting point for offering a responsive program. Every stage of development is an exciting period of growth and learning. Think about a 2-year-old in your program. She loves opening and closing cupboard doors and insists that you read *Goodnight Moon* to her a dozen times in a row. The 4-year-old in your program enjoys using paper, markers, and crayons. Knowing that these are typical behaviors enables you to respond in meaningful and appropriate ways. The *Creative Curriculum for Family Child Care* illustrates various ideas and strategies by giving examples that involve the seven imaginary children who are introduced below.

Infants (Birth–18 Months)

Jeremy is 8 months old now and has been in family child care since he was 6 weeks old. He has just learned to crawl and is beginning to pull himself up to a standing position. He loves playing peek-a-boo and laughs heartily whenever you uncover your face. He babbles constantly, saying, "Da-da-ba-ba," and experimenting with other strings of sounds and with various intonations.

Babies must have their basic needs met by adults they can trust. Once their basic needs are met, they become eager explorers who use all of their senses to examine objects within reach. They are fascinated by people and soon learn to smile and interact with them. As babies learn more about people and as they handle objects, they acquire new skills.

Knowing what infants are like will help you to meet their needs and nurture their development and learning. The chart below lists some of the major aspects of infant development and indicates how this knowledge supports you in planning a responsive program.

Aspects of Infants' Development	How to Use This Knowledge
Socially and emotionally, infants…	*As a provider, you…*
depend on adults to meet their basic needs (to be fed, kept dry, kept warm and cool enough, kept healthy, put to sleep, picked up, held, cuddled, played with, and comforted).	respond to each child individually, building the child's trust and sense of security. Once babies trust you, they feel safe to explore the environment.
form strong attachments to the important people in their lives.	offer consistent, responsive care for all infants. Children who are cared for and nurtured consistently are more likely to feel confident and become independent.

Aspects of Infants' Development	How to Use This Knowledge
like to watch other children and be part of the action.	talk about what other children are doing: "Tamika is beating the drum. We can do that, too." Include infants in activities, such as finger painting with pudding while other children are using paint.
Physically, infants…	*As a provider you…*
explore and move by rolling over, sitting, creeping, crawling, pulling themselves up, cruising, and walking.	arrange floor space so that there is a large space for babies to move about freely and safely. Provide sturdy furniture and railings so they can pull themselves up.
are developing small-muscle skills such as touching, grasping, patting, and grabbing.	provide opportunities for infants to develop a pincer grasp (holding objects with the thumb and index finger) and other small-muscle skills.
In terms of language, infants…	*As a provider you…*
understand many words long before they can speak.	talk to babies, sing with them, and read to them throughout the day. Their brains are primed for learning language, so talk and encourage their attempts to imitate speech.
communicate first by babbling and through gestures and facial expressions and then by speaking.	respond to babies' gestures, smiles, and coos. Start a "conversation" with them, even if they only respond with a smile or a coo.
begin to learn the names of objects in their environment.	encourage children to repeat speech sounds and words as you converse.
Cognitively, infants…	*As a provider you…*
use their five senses to explore the world.	make sure that the infant toys and objects in your home are safe to be mouthed, squeezed, shaken, and tossed.

Aspects of Infants' Development	How to Use This Knowledge
hold and manipulate objects, discovering the effects of their actions.	encourage infants to explore and experiment with toys and materials. Comment on what you see and hear: "Marta, when you raised your bottle, you got every last drop of milk out of it."
begin to understand that objects and people exist even when they are out of sight.	play games such as peek-a-boo to help infants learn that people and objects are still somewhere, even when they are not visible. This concept is known as "object permanence." Understanding it is a developmental milestone.

Toddlers and Twos (18–36 Months)

Tamika, who is 19 months old, is a sociable toddler. Two of her favorite activities are water play and digging in sand. Tamika is just starting to talk and speaks in two-word phrases. Her favorite expressions are "Me do!" and "No." She picks up books to look at on her own, but she especially enjoys being read to and turning the pages, herself. Her older brother is Tyrone, who is 8 years old.

Jorge is a determined 2 ½-year-old. He is in constant motion, running to do everything. Jorge is a dual-language learner. He is learning Spanish at home and English in family child care. He often mixes the two languages, for example, saying, "Mas milk," or "Quiero ball." Some days he speaks mostly Spanish, but he understands more and more English every day.

Children of this age are very active from the moment they awaken. Toddlers walk, run, hop, throw balls, and even pedal tricycles. They know how to put large pegs in a pegboard, snap beads into a chain, and pour water from a child-sized pitcher into a cup. Twos make purposeful marks on paper, pound and poke playdough, and repeatedly build towers to knock down. The world is an exciting place for toddlers and twos, but it can also be overwhelming. Sometimes they want the impossible: to be big and to stay little at the same time. The same child who says, "Me do!" when you try to help him wash his hands may want you to cuddle him like a baby 5 minutes later. Toddlers and twos want and need to practice their new skills, make their own decisions, and do things themselves, even though those things do not always work out the way they would like them to.

Aspects of Toddlers' and Twos' Development	How to Use This Knowledge
Socially and emotionally, toddlers and twos...	*As a provider, you...*
assert themselves and want to do things independently.	provide a safe way for them to practice self-help skills (for example, handwashing, nose blowing, and toothbrushing) as independently as they can. Offer simple puzzles, foam blocks, sturdy books, and water-based markers that children can use successfully on their own.
are beginning to learn about taking turns and waiting, but sharing is still difficult for them.	provide opportunities for children to learn to take turns. Provide duplicates of favorite toys so children can play with them at the same time.
are starting to use caring behaviors to help and comfort others.	model caring behaviors and acknowledge children's behavior whenever you see them caring for others.
Physically, toddlers and twos...	*As a provider, you...*
can push themselves around on wheeled toys, walk easily, run, jump, and hop.	create an environment with safe spaces for children to run and ride wheeled toys freely. Plan music and movement activities every day to promote children's physical development.
gain small-muscle skills such as turning pages, drawing with crayons, opening containers, and popping beads together and apart.	give children lots of opportunities to play with toys, puzzles, and other manipulatives. Keep your program stocked with art and writing materials that encourage small-muscle development.

Aspects of Toddlers' and Twos' Development	How to Use This Knowledge
In terms of language, toddlers and twos...	*As a provider, you...*
are increasing their listening and speaking vocabularies rapidly.	introduce new vocabulary by naming objects, actions, and feelings and by using descriptive words. Speak in complete sentences and in a clear, even voice.
communicate in short, two- or three-word sentences (for example, "Dat mine" or "Mommy go now.").	engage children in many conversations. This will give them opportunities to learn to express their thoughts and feelings.
enjoy books with rhymes, predictable words and phrases, and colorful illustrations.	provide unhurried time to read books with one or two children at a time. Encourage them to point to and name pictures. Ask questions and relate the stories to the children's lives.
Cognitively, toddlers and twos...	*As a provider, you...*
like to practice new skills by using them again and again.	provide opportunities for children to participate in familiar experiences as often as they would like.
enjoy imitating and pretending.	provide dramatic play clothing, props, and furnishings that encourage children to explore familiar roles and to play together. Offer children opportunities to do adult-like things, such as cooking, sorting laundry, and cleaning up after themselves.
are beginning to understand basic concepts about sequence and the order of daily events.	use a daily schedule to help children learn that there is a predictable order to the day. This helps children feel safe and learn about sequencing.

Preschool Children (3–5 Years)

Nathan, age 3, is an outgoing child who is often frustrated by his inability to communicate. He uses a variety of language sounds and uses a few single words, but he rarely strings them together in phrases or sentences. Nathan has been diagnosed as having a language delay. As part of his therapy, a speech therapist visits him while he is at your family child care program.

Rosa, age 4, was born in Mexico and recently moved to the United States with her family. She speaks Spanish and is just beginning to understand and speak English. She was quiet at first, but she has developed a friendship with Keisha and now seems much more comfortable in the program. She offers to help the younger children, volunteering to help feed Jeremy and look at books with Tamika and Jorge.

Keisha is 4 ½ years old. In our imaginary family child care home, she is your daughter. When you first started your program, Keisha was 8 months old. She is now very accustomed to having other children in her home. She is an eager learner, can read the names of all of the children at FCC, and knows how to write her own name. She loves dressing up in grown-up clothes to play house, and she enjoys making colorful collages. She especially loves to look at books and have them read to her.

Think of preschool children as scientists who are interested in understanding and mastering the world around them. They are curious about everything, theorizing about how things work, making predictions, and trying their ideas. They develop valuable social skills, including cooperation, empathy, responsibility, and a desire to resolve social conflicts. Their large-motor skills have progressed and become more complex. By the end of the preschool years, most children speak their home languages fluently and are developing early reading and writing skills.

Aspects of Preschool Children's Development	How to Use This Knowledge
Socially and emotionally, preschool children...	*As a provider, you...*
are learning to solve social problems through negotiation and compromise.	engage children in a social problem solving process.
like to play with other children and often have one or two best friends.	provide opportunities for children to play together. Encourage children to help each other, to cooperate on tasks, and to comfort other children. Support children as they learn to make friends.
are able to recognize, name, and express their feelings and those of others.	encourage children to label and talk about their emotions. Relate the feelings of storybook characters to the children's own lives. Emphasize the importance of respecting both their own and others' feelings.
Physically, preschool children...	*As a provider, you...*
are refining large-muscle skills by running, jumping, kicking, hopping, galloping, pedaling, climbing, throwing, and catching.	plan movement experiences and obstacle courses indoors. Outdoors, make sure the space and equipment are adequate for running, jumping, climbing, constructing, playing games with balls and hoops, riding a trike, pulling a wagon, or using a scooter. Be sure to provide helmets so that children can play safely.
increase their fine motor skills and eye–hand coordination.	offer children materials to support fine-motor development. Provide experiences such as stringing beads, working with clay and playdough, measuring cooking ingredients, and using the computer keyboard and mouse.

Aspects of Preschool Children's Development	How to Use This Knowledge
In terms of language, preschool children…	*As a provider, you…*
can speak in complete sentences.	engage children in conversations and model grammatically correct language. Pose open-ended questions that require more than a *yes* or *no* answer.
begin to write letters and words.	provide children with many opportunities to write (for example, on sign-up sheets, on artwork, in thank-you letters, and in dramatic play.) Provide writing materials where children can sit at a table while they explore writing.
enjoy a variety of books (stories and nonfiction) and may have favorites.	encourage families and children to bring their favorite books. Make trips to your public library, enroll the children in a book club, or get a subscription to a children's magazine. Build your library through yard sales and donations.
Cognitively, preschool children…	*As a provider, you…*
are curious about how things work and what they can do.	help children conduct in-depth investigations of meaningful topics that they want to learn more about. Ask children about their observations and predictions, posing questions to extend their thinking.
are able to match, sort, classify, compare, use numbers, and make patterns.	give children many opportunities to count objects, develop an understanding of one-to-one correspondence, sort and classify objects, compare, and measure.
connect new experiences and ideas with what they already know.	point out connections and encourage children to make these links. For example, ask, "What other plants have we grown that we were able to eat?"

School-Age Children (6–12 Years)

Tyrone, age 8, is a school-age child who has been in the program since you started offering care. He views this as his second home, especially because his younger sister, Tamika, began coming to your program. Tyrone is doing well in school and likes to do his homework when he arrives. He usually still has time to play with the other children.

School-age children have many experiences away from their homes and your program. When they are at your program, they want a supportive place where they can relax, communicate with a caring adult, perhaps work on a project of interest, and do their homework. School-age children are beginning to think and reason logically and to approach problems with greater flexibility and efficiency. Despite their growing sense of independence, it is important to remember that they are still children who need supervision without overprotection. Your FCC home can provide a safe and welcoming place for children before and after school and during school holidays, vacations, and family emergencies.

Aspects of School-Age Children's Development	How to Use This Knowledge
Socially and emotionally, school-age children…	*As a provider, you…*
are eager to be independent from adults.	give children opportunities to play on their own, study, and be with peers. Let them help themselves to nutritious snacks and tell them when they need to check in with you. Encourage them to help younger children.
are concerned about being accepted by peers, and they often conform to peer expectations.	create an environment where all children feel as though they are part of the FCC group and where their unique abilities and interests are promoted. Make each child feel special. At the same time, give children opportunities to share experiences with their peers that are acceptable to you and their families.

Aspects of School-Age Children's Development	How to Use This Knowledge
enjoy cooperative games and games with rules, but they may have difficulty with losing.	offer physical activities through which school-age children can refine their motor skills. When children feel discouraged, invite them to talk about their feelings and plan ways to strengthen their skills.
Physically, school-age children…	*As a provider, you…*
enjoy participating in activities such as swimming, skating, riding bikes, doing gymnastics, jumping rope, and playing games of their own design, but they are not always as coordinated as they would like to be.	provide children with space, time, and the appropriate equipment so they can refine their large-muscle skills. Enhance activities by encouraging children to play with their peers.
able to use fine-motor skills to complete complex tasks.	provide many opportunities to draw, paint, weave, sculpt, play musical instruments, complete puzzles, and work on woodworking or other craft projects.
In terms of language, school-age children…	*As a provider, you…*
are fluent in their home languages and able to express their ideas and feelings verbally.	encourage children to write, read, and perform their plays for the other children. Converse with children, asking open-ended questions to encourage them to talk about their ideas and feelings in detail.
enjoy learning new words and like to describe things in intricate detail.	provide lots of books with interesting vocabulary. Converse with children and challenge them to elaborate on their descriptions.

Aspects of School-Age Children's Development	How to Use This Knowledge
are increasingly skilled and interested in reading, speaking, and writing.	provide opportunities for children to make books, use the computer for reading and writing, and read stories (including reading aloud to younger children). Stock your FCC home with books and magazines of interest to school-age children.
Cognitively, school-age children…	*As a provider, you…*
enjoy working on long-term projects and like to make finished products.	work with children to conduct long-term studies that interest them. Encourage children to identify and verbalize their questions, do research, experiment, and represent their ideas.
like to use their imaginations.	provide lots of materials and ideas to encourage children to be creative. They can do art or woodworking projects, write plays for the other children to perform, make something special in the kitchen, or write their own stories. Remember that everything they do is an expression of their imaginations. There are no right or wrong ways for children to use their imaginations.

Objectives for Development and Learning: Birth to Age 6

To provide a high-quality program in your family child care home, you need to know how children develop and what you want them to learn. It is useful to think about child development and learning in terms of four areas: social–emotional, cognitive, language, and physical development. These four areas are closely related and often overlap. Development in one area affects and is influenced by development in all other areas.

In *The Creative Curriculum*, the objectives for development and learning address the important aspects of young children's development. They guide your observations and the decisions you make as you plan, offer learning experiences, and otherwise provide responsive care. In this chapter, we present the objectives that are related to children's general development and learning. In chapter 3, "What Children Are Learning," we present the objectives for children's learning in the content areas of literacy, math, science, social studies, and the arts. In chapter 4, we talk about how to use the objectives as you guide children's progress.

The following section provides an overview of the four areas of child development and presents the curricular objectives that are related to each developmental area. Please note that they are objectives for children younger than age 6. Objectives for school-age children are specified by the curricula used in their schools and by state learning standards.

Social–emotional development involves the way children feel about themselves, their understanding of feelings, their ability to regulate emotions and express them appropriately, and their capacity for building relationships with others. *The Creative Curriculum* has three objectives for social–emotional development:

Objective 1. Regulates own emotions and behaviors

Objective 2. Establishes and sustains positive relationships

Objective 3. Participates cooperatively and constructively in group situations

Physical development includes children's gross (large muscle) and fine (small muscle) motor skills. These skills progress in a fairly typical pattern from simple to complex. As children gain physical skills, they are more and more able to do self-care tasks such as feeding and dressing themselves. *The Creative Curriculum* includes has four objectives for physical development:

Objective 4. Demonstrates traveling skills

Objective 5. Demonstrates balancing skills

Objective 6. Demonstrates gross motor manipulative skills

Objective 7. Demonstrates fine-motor strength and coordination

Oral language development includes children's ability to listen; to understand; and to express thoughts, needs, and ideas. Oral language development is closely tied to literacy, the ability to read and write. Strong oral language and literacy skills are essential for children's success in school and in life. (Literacy objectives are addressed in chapter 3, "What Children Are Learning.") *The Creative Curriculum* includes three objectives for oral language development:

Objective 8. Listens to and understands increasingly complex language

Objective 9. Uses spoken language to express thoughts and needs

Objective 10. Uses appropriate conversational and other communication skills

Cognitive development involves the way children think, approach learning, develop understandings about the world, and use what they learn to solve problems. *The Creative Curriculum* includes four objectives for cognitive development.

Objective 11. Demonstrates positive approaches to learning

Objective 12. Remembers and connects experiences

Objective 13. Classifies and sorts

Objective 14. Uses symbols and images to represent something not present

Individual Differences

While knowing about typical child development helps you know what children of a particular age or stage are like in general, it is only by understanding individual differences that you can respond appropriately to the children in your care. What motivates her? What comforts him when he is distressed? To what foods is she allergic? On what strengths can you help him build? What challenges should you consider? As a family child care provider, you are in a unique position to get to know each child in your program very well. By observing children regularly and talking with their families, you can learn what makes each child unique.

You should consider a number of individual differences as you plan your program. This section examines four of the most important considerations.

Life Circumstances

Each child has different life experiences. Is he or she an only child? Is there a new baby in the family? Think about how each of the following factors affect the children in your program but remember not to generalize or make judgments about families on the basis of their life circumstances.

- the family's composition
- the family's cultural practices
- the language the family speaks at home
- the community where the family lives
- the family's history of moving
- the type of work and level of education of family members
- socioeconomic status
- hours of parental employment
- special circumstances such as marital separation, divorce, or deployment
- presence of a chronic physical or mental health problem, including addiction or recovery from addiction, or a family member's disability
- exposure to violence, abuse, or neglect

Families may or may not feel comfortable sharing information about their life circumstances when they first enroll their child in your program. As they get to know and trust you, they may feel more comfortable with this, or they may still prefer not to share such personal information. Respect each family's privacy. Families also have a right to be certain that any information they share with you will remain confidential. If families share information with you that you do not know how to handle, seek advice from an outside expert to support you and the family.

Encourage families to communicate with you about anything new taking place in their lives. A pending move to a new home, a new baby, or a divorce is likely to change a child's immediate behavior as well as his life in a more comprehensive sense. A child who comes from a home where a sibling has a disability may feel as though his or her own needs are not being met because the family's attention and resources are concentrated on the sibling. When you know that Rosa's family recently moved from Mexico and that she misses her "abuela," you can ask her family to bring pictures of their home and family in Mexico. You might also send home a picture that Rosa drew so her family can send it to her grandmother.

How to Use This Knowledge

- Take the time to develop a relationship with and get to know families. Invite them to share information as they feel comfortable.

- Provide materials and plan experiences that relate to what you know about each child. For example, Rosa might enjoy hearing about Ana Patino, who did not speak English when her family moved to the United States from Mexico.

- Talk about many kinds of families. Read Cheryl Boeller's *Do I Have a Daddy?*, which is about a single-parent family, or Nikki Grimes' *Oh, Brother*, which is about a child who is not so sure that he likes having a new stepbrother.

- Respond constructively to changes in a child's behavior that are related to a change in circumstances or to family stress.

- Be aware of community resources for families who are having difficulty coping with life circumstances. Offer information if asked to do so.

Temperament

All of us are born with a behavioral style called *temperament*. For example, some children approach new situations cautiously and adapt slowly, some children withdraw or cry, and others are generally cheerful about encountering something unfamiliar. Being aware of a child's temperament means you may be able to anticipate his reaction and prepare the child for what is ahead. Tamika and Nathan may become engaged in a new activity more quickly than Rosa, who tends to watch before becoming actively involved. Consider the following temperament-related questions to help you get to know and plan for each child in your program:[1]

- How active is he? Does he watch, listen, or manipulate everything?

- Are her sleeping and eating habits predictable? Does she always wake up hungry? Does she nap at the same time every day?

- How does he react to change? How long does it take him to get used to new foods, new people, and other new experiences?

- Do changes in noise, light, or temperature bother her? Does wearing certain textures of clothing bother her? Is she sensitive to any foods?

- Does he have a positive or negative outlook? Is he generally in a light-hearted mood, or does he take things very seriously?

- How does she react emotionally? Does she react loudly and dramatically to even the most minor disappointment, or does she become quiet when she is upset?

- How long does he stay with a task when it is challenging? How does he react to interruptions or requests to clean up when he is playing?

Children with different temperaments respond to situations differently. Thinking about temperament helps you understand each child's behavior so you can act in ways that best meet his or her needs. As you learn about the individual temperaments of the children in your care, you may need to adjust the way in which you support that child. In addition, your own temperament may affect the ways you respond to children in your care. Sometimes temperaments challenge us because they are different from our own. At other times, we find behaviors challenging because they are similar to our own approach to situations. Awareness of your own temperament can help you understand your reactions to children's behaviors. Temperament may be inborn, but you can support an active child by calming her or support a child who tends to withdraw by showing him how to enter a group activity.

How to Use This Knowledge

- Be aware of your own temperament and those of the children in your group. Are you a quiet person who is a bit overwhelmed by a boisterous child? Are you an outgoing person who sometimes overlooks a quiet child? Think about how your responses to children are affected by the differences between your temperament and theirs. When you find a child's behavior challenging, think about whether you can change your practices, environment, or schedule to support the child. For example, could you make a calm, soothing place in your FCC home for a child who is sensitive to light and colors?

- Help a child who tends to withdraw learn strategies for entering a group and for making friends. Give the child language to use, for example, "May I help build your house?" or "Would you like to use my crayons?"

- Help a child who is quick to react learn techniques to slow down. For example, coach, "Take a deep breath and count to ten."

Home Language

It's very likely that you have—or will have—a child whose home language is not English. We often refer to children who speak a language other than English at home and who are learning English as *dual-language learners*. You may speak some children's home languages, but you may not speak everyone's. If you and all of the children in your program speak the same language, you may choose to speak only that language in your FCC home.

Some dual-language learners, especially children under age 3, like Jorge, are learning two languages at the same time. They are learning English and their family's home language. These children are learning two languages simultaneously. Other children, especially preschool-age children like Rosa, already speak their family's home language and are beginning to learn English while in your care. This is an example of sequential language acquisition. All but newborn children come to your program with some knowledge about language and its uses. However, some arrive with strong home language skills while others are still developing a foundation on which to build language skills. No matter what the circumstance, all children need a language-rich environment while they are in your care. In chapter 4, "Caring and Teaching," and throughout the chapters on routines and experiences, we offer specific suggestions for supporting children who are learning two languages.

If both languages are supported equally, children who are learning two languages develop both languages by following the same process as a child who is learning one language. Once they begin to speak, they may mix the two languages, using words from both languages to express a thought. This is known as *code switching*. Code switching is very common for both children and adults who know more than one language, especially when they are speaking to others who speak both languages. When speaking to people who speak only one language, children eventually separate the languages and learn to speak to people in the appropriate language. For example, Rosa is likely to speak to her parents in Spanish and her English-speaking family child care provider in English.

Patton Tabors identifies four stages through which dual-language learners progress. Like all language learners, these children typically understand more words than they can speak. The following chart outlines each stage and what you might observe at each stage.

Stages of Learning a Second Language[2]

Stages	What You Might Observe
Home Language Use	Children continue to use their home languages with teachers and other children, even if they are not understood.
Nonverbal Period	Children limit (or stop) the use of their home languages as they realize that their speech is not understood by others. This period can last from a few months to a year. Children may use gestures or pantomime to express their needs, usually to get attention, make a request, protest, or joke.
Telegraphic and Formulaic Speech	Children begin using one- and two-word phrases in English, especially to name objects. They may use groups of words such as "Stop it," "Fall down," or "Shut up," although they may not always use them appropriately.
Productive Use of Language	Children begin to use simple sentences they have heard in English, and they begin to form their own sentences by using words in new combinations. Like all young children, they gradually increase the length of their sentences.

Many factors, such as a child's temperament, amount of previous experience with English, and opportunities to use English, influence how quickly a child moves through each stage and develops expressive language skills in English. For example, with her quiet temperament, Rosa may stay in the nonverbal stage longer than a child who is more outgoing.

It is important for you to model grammatically correct English and to encourage the children's families to speak and read to them in their home languages. Bring the children's home languages into your program as much as you are comfortable doing. Research about Spanish-speaking children has shown that teachers who speak even a little bit of Spanish to them promote the social skills that support learning a new language.[3]

How to Use This Knowledge

- Remember that understanding comes before speaking. Whether the child is responding in his or her home language or going through a nonverbal or early speech period, remember that the child may understand quite a lot of what you say.

- Children show their development and learning in many ways that do not involve spoken language. Watch how children who are learning English play with materials, how they interact with other children, and how they move. Remember that skills that are learned in a child's first language transfer to their second language.

- Support families in speaking their home languages with their children. Explain why it is important for children to continue to learn and speak their home languages while they learn English.

Disabilities

All children have strengths and needs of varying kinds. Some children have special needs because they have disabilities. While there are many types of disabilities, most can be described as developmental delays and medical, emotional, or physical problems. Increasing numbers of children are being identified as having attention-related disorders and autism.

Always think of children with disabilities as children first. Learn about each child's strengths and interests and then consider the child's special challenges. Remember that a disability is only one aspect of a child's development. It does not define the whole child. Children with disabilities have a wide-range of abilities and needs. A child may have a disability that affects one area of development, but he or she may be developing typically in other developmental areas. Children with disabilities usually follow the same pattern as children who are developing typically. However, they may develop at a slower pace, in a different sequence, or take smaller steps toward a developmental objective.

The first questions about a child's need for special services may be raised at the child's birth, during a later medical checkup, by the family, by a specialist, or by you. As a family child care provider, you may be the first person to become concerned about a child's development. Federal law requires each state to have a Child Find system to help identify children with disabilities and make sure that they receive appropriate services. If you are concerned about a child's development, talk with the child's family and help them learn how to access the local Child Find system.

Two federal laws govern services provided to young children with disabilities. One law governs services for children under age 3. The other specifies services for older children. Both laws require the development of a plan that answers basic questions about the nature of the child's disability and specifies what must be done to meet his educational needs. For children under age 3, the law requires the creation of an Individualized Family Service Plan (IFSP). Services must be provided in a "natural setting." A natural setting is one in which the child would spend time if he or she did not have a disability. This definition makes a family child care home an ideal setting for a child with disabilities. For children age 3 and above, the law requires that a child with a diagnosed disability who is eligible for special education services have an Individualized Education Program (IEP). The IFSP and IEP include goals and objectives, a description of how the disability affects the child's access to the general curriculum, and the types of special education services the child needs.

In addition to these two laws, the Americans with Disabilities Act (ADA) requires family child care homes and centers to make reasonable modifications to include children with disabilities. To meet the law's provisions, FCC providers must make simple, inexpensive changes, such as getting rid of physical barriers or providing adaptive equipment.

Special education legislation ensures that children with disabilities, their families, and their family child care providers are supported well. If a child in your FCC program has a diagnosed disability, the child's IFSP or IEP will identify the type and frequency of the services he or she needs. For example, if a child has a chronic medical condition, health care workers will assist you in learning to feed the child and provide medication. Additional service providers may include speech therapists, occupational therapists, or physical therapists. All of these specialists will provide services in the natural environment of your family child care home and help you include the child with disabilities in all aspects of your program.

How to Use This Knowledge

- Think about children as children first, for example, as a "child with mental retardation," not "a mentally retarded child." Learn about the whole child. For example, find out what Nathan likes to do. Learn about his favorite toys and books, not just about his language delay.

- Talk with families about becoming part of their child's IFSP or IEP team.

- Welcome a child's service providers (for example, speech and language pathologists, and physical and occupational therapists) to your family child care home. Help them to understand how you work with children. Encourage them to include the other children in your program in the activities that they provide for a child with disabilities.

- Learn any special techniques you should use with the child with disabilities and ways to include the child in everything that you do in your family child care home.

Summary

In your family child care program, you may care for infants, toddlers, twos, and preschool and school-age children. To understand how to organize your home and your day; what children are learning; and how to guide their behavior, learning, and progress, you need to have a good understanding of what children are generally like at each stage of development and what developmental objectives to keep in mind. Understanding individual differences helps you remember that each child is unique and that life circumstances, temperament, home language, and the presence of a disability affect children's development.

[1] Chess, S., & Thomas, A. (1996). *Temperament: Theory and practice.* New York: Bruner/Mazel.

[2] Tabors, P. O. (2008). *One child, two languages* (2nd ed.). Baltimore, MD: Paul H. Brookes Publishing.

[3] Chang, F., Crawford, G., Early, D., Bryant, C., Howes, M., Burchinal, O., Barbarin, R., Clifford, R., & Pianta, R. (2007). Spanish–speaking children's social and language development in pre-kindergarten classrooms. *Journal of Early Education and Development, 18*(2), 243–69.

Organizing Your Home and Your Day

2

Organizing Your Home and Your Day

A family child care home is a unique environment for early childhood education. Part home and part child care program, it provides a relaxed environment for learning. However, the combination also poses special challenges. Providers meet these challenges in different ways. Some providers take advantage of the home's familiar environment for their program. They use the living room, with its comfortable couch and chairs for reading and snuggling. They use the kitchen, where they can cook; serve meals; and let children play with pots, pans, and plastic containers. The bathroom becomes a place to smile, sing, and talk with children so that diapering and toileting are times to build relationships and support learning. Other FCC providers prefer to designate a separate space in their home. That space is used only for family child care, not for their families. Both models have strengths and challenges, so some providers use a combination of separate and shared space. To help you select the arrangement that works best for you and your family, these approaches are discussed below.

This chapter provides general information about creating an indoor environment that meets the needs of the children in your program as well as your family's needs. It also includes information about planning a responsive program. Chapters 6–20 provide specific information about arranging the environment for daily routines and experiences.

This chapter includes three sections:

Setting Up Your Home discusses options for arranging your home for family child care. These include shared space, separate space, or a combination of the two. It includes information about how to furnish, equip, and organize your family child care home so that it is safe and welcoming for children and families. It explains how to arrange the environment to encourage positive behavior, and it suggests ways to store and display materials so that children can use and care for them easily.

Planning Your Day talks about how to develop a flexible daily schedule that helps structure the day's routines and experiences. It discusses the events of the day and shows how to plan so that your program runs smoothly.

Planning Your Week explains more about thinking ahead. It introduces the "Child Planning Form" and the "Group Planning Form," which help you use what you know about the children in your group to plan meaningful play experiences.

Setting Up Your Home

The way you arrange your family child care home can make it easier for children to learn, get along with others, and become independent. It can encourage positive behavior. It can also make it easier for you to care for children.

Many factors influence the way you set up your home for family child care. These include such considerations as the size of your home, whether you have a basement or another large room to set aside for the FCC program, and the type of flooring in your home. You also need to think about whether you have a safe place for children to play outdoors or whether you will take them to a nearby playground or park. Some family child care providers use areas throughout their homes during the day and convert the spaces back into family living areas at the end of the day. They store equipment in closets and move heavy items on wheels. Others designate parts of their home for family child care and always leave them set up that way. Your decisions will depend on the size and design of your home, as well as your family's feelings about sharing space. Many providers use a combination. For example, they reserve a family room in the basement exclusively for family child care but also use the kitchen and bedrooms as family child care space.

Here are some things to think about as you choose the arrangement that is best for you and your family:

- Is your family comfortable with sharing space? How will your own children feel about having other children in their space?

- Does your home have space that can be dedicated to family child care without taking away needed family space?

- Will you enjoy having your family space filled with children? Are you comfortable with removing your favorite knickknacks because they are breakable or you do not want children to handle them? Would you prefer to reserve your living room for your family's use, keeping it as a place where you can retreat in comfort at the end of a child-filled day?

- Are you comfortable with the smudges that children's messy activities might bring to your home, or will you be more comfortable if these activities are held in a separate space?

Shared Space

A home can be a stimulating but relaxed environment for learning. There are soft and safe places for children to explore. You may have plants and pets for which the children can help care. The kitchen is made for cooking activities and meals. The carpet or rug in your living room can be a place for "tummy time" for a young infant and a place where two preschool children can play a simple board game. Common kitchen equipment, such as wooden spoons to bang on pots, or measuring cups to nest, make wonderful toys for children. Sharing your family space makes children feel comfortable almost immediately, and this homey environment is often one of the things that families are looking for when they choose family child care rather than center care.

When the place that is used to care for children is also your family's home, you have to consider not only the needs of your family child care children but also your own needs and those of your family. Balancing needs can be a challenge, so you must think about how to convert your home into program space during the day and turn it back into a space that your family uses and enjoys after family child care hours.

The following guidelines will help you use shared family child care space effectively:

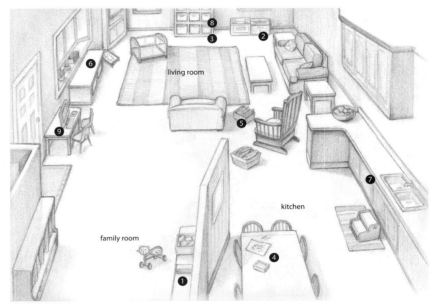

1. Blocks
2. Dramatic Play
3. Toys and Games
4. Art
5. Library
6. Discovery
7. Sand and Water
8. Music and Movement
9. Computers

Identify which rooms of your home will be used for family child care and which are off-limits to the children. Decide where experiences can take place in your home. Is your living room a large space that can be used for active musical games, block building, and dramatic play? Will you offer water play in the kitchen or perhaps the bathroom? Look for comfortable places for quiet activities such as looking at books, drawing with crayons, and listening to music.

Close off places that are off-limits. For example, a tool shed or storage area can be locked, and your bedroom door can be closed. Rooms that you do not wish to use for your program can be blocked by a door, a gate, or a large piece of furniture. Childproof the space used by children. Breakable objects can be stored in areas that are off-limits.

Set aside a place for school-age children to be by themselves when they want and where you keep their games and special materials such as paper, scissors, markers, and glue.

Make taking out and putting away family child care materials as easy as possible. Identify storages spaces where FCC materials can be out of sight and mind after program hours. Put FCC materials in wheeled carts so they can be moved easily.

Separate Space

If you reserve places in your home only for your family child care program, you can designate experience areas for particular types of play. For example, children need a

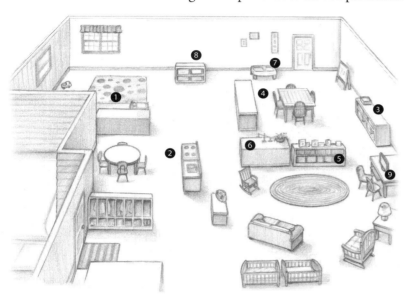

protected space for playing with blocks, an easy-to-clean area for messy activities such as art or water play, and some cozy spots for reading or listening to music. A couch, armchair, rug, and curtains make the program space comfortable for you and the children.

The amount of space in your home will determine how many areas you can set up. Here are some arrangement guidelines:

Separate noisy areas from quiet ones.

Define each area clearly by using shelves, tables, or tape so children can identify physical boundaries easily.

Locate experience areas near needed resources. For example, set up art materials near a water source, and place a computer and CD player near electrical outlets.

1. Blocks
2. Dramatic Play
3. Toys and Games
4. Art
5. Library
6. Discovery
7. Sand and Water
8. Music and Movement
9. Computers

General Considerations

As you can see, both shared-space and separate-space options for setting up a family child care home have pros and cons. Providers select the options that work best in their spaces and for their families. In addition, some providers think that family child care programs should take full advantage of the home setting, while others think that it is better to have an atmosphere that is more like school. Here are some guidelines that apply to all family child care models:

Make your environment welcoming to the children and families. Add decorative touches such as nontoxic plants, colorful table mats, textured pillows, and perhaps a well-lit fish tank. Encourage families to bring photos, and place them where children can see them.

Locate a greeting area just inside the entrance to your home. It will be a transitional area between the outdoors and the inside of your home. Children can store their belongings there, and you can make families feel welcome with a bulletin board for messages and family photos.

Make the environment comfortable and convenient for you and other adults. Minimize physical strain whenever possible. For example, put durable cushioned mats in front of the kitchen sink or other places where you stand for a long time. An armrest reduces strain when bottle-feeding infants. You might want to keep a small long-handled dustpan and broom handy so you can pick up small toys from the floor without bending. Have comfortable adult seating throughout your home.

Make cleanup as easy as possible. Put a plastic shower curtain on the floor to contain spills. Feed children in areas where the floor is washable.

Organize storage areas to find things easily and remain attentive to the children. Find spaces to keep adult tools, such as scissors and knives, handy for you but out of the children's reach. Think about where to store your first-aid kit and identify places both in and out of the refrigerator to store medications.

Identify a place where a sick child can wait comfortably to be picked up by his or her family member.

When necessary, arrange the environment to accommodate a child with a disability. Most of the furnishings and equipment in your home are appropriate for children with disabilities. However, you may need to rearrange them and have a place to keep adaptive equipment. Families may provide special equipment, such as seating and positioning equipment, and orientation and mobility devices designed specifically for the child's size and needs. If the child has an Individualized Family Service Plan (IFSP) or Individualized Education Program (IEP), the special equipment will probably be specified in the document. Family members and physical or occupational therapists who work with the child can show you how to use the equipment.

Here are some examples of accommodations for children with disabilities:

- If a child uses a wheelchair or walker, you may need a ramp to your home, and you might need to install grab bars in the bathroom. You may also need to make other simple changes, such as rearranging furniture to allow a child to maneuver a wheelchair.

- To participate fully in the program, some children with physical disabilities need support when they sit and stand. A large cushion can be adjusted to provide support while the child is sitting.

- Use a variety of textures to differentiate areas for a child who is blind. For example, define one area with a rug and another with a foam mat. A large inflatable wading pool can provide a safe play space for a very young child.

- A child with may respond negatively to bright lights and loud sounds. Use as much natural light as possible. Add dimmers and put on background music if it soothes the child.

- A child may use an alternative communication system or device to help him or her express needs, feelings, and ideas. Have the family and the speech therapist explain how the child uses it.

Keeping Children Safe

Whether your family child care program is located in a space used only for family child care or takes place throughout your home, safety is the first consideration. In a family child care home, you—and you alone—are responsible for the safety of the children in your care. Supervision is critical. The National Association for Family Child Care safety standards require that providers be able to see or hear all children at all times. Children under age 5 may not be left inside or outside by themselves. Children younger than age 3 must be in the provider's sight at all times, except when the provider is attending to his or her personal needs for as many as 5 minutes. When children age 3 or older are not in sight, providers must be able to hear them.[1]

Childproofing your home to eliminate dangers and potential accidents is a vital step in preparing your home for children. A safe environment enables children to explore, satisfy their curiosity, and learn through play. Your choice and organization of materials and equipment can prevent accidents. In a safe environment, you can encourage children to explore instead of worrying about possible injuries.

One of the challenges of maintaining a safe environment in a family child care home is meeting the needs of a diverse group that may include infants, toddlers, twos, preschool children, and school-age children. Your knowledge of child development will help you think about how to set up the environment. For example, if infants are in your care, you need a protected space where they can play on the floor without getting run over by an older child. You also need a place where older children can play actively without tripping over babies. A toy that is appropriate for a 4-year-old can be a choking hazard for an infant or toddler. Safety concerns change as children develop, so your environment may need to change as young infants become mobile and as toddlers become preschoolers. Assess your environment frequently as well as when you begin caring for a new child. Make any changes needed to keep children safe.

Some safety hazards are unique to family child care programs because they are in a home setting. Fireplaces and firearms, for instance, are rarely found in a child care center, but they are in some family child care homes. Bathroom and bedroom doors may have locks. Although child care centers often have pet rabbits, guinea pigs, hamsters, or gerbils, they rarely have dogs or cats. Use a safety checklist to identify hazards in both your indoor and outdoor environments.

Here are some additional safety guidelines:

Be aware of ongoing safety hazards. For instance, always keep pot handles turned toward the back of the stove when you are cooking so children cannot grab them and pull pots down on themselves. Make sure that you always put away sharp scissors and knives. Keep matches, plastic bags, and pocketbooks out of children's reach. Lock away medications, cleaning materials, and other toxic substances.

Check some things every day. Before you take children outdoors, make sure that your yard is free of trash, broken glass, and animal waste. Check that outlets are covered and that the child safety locks on cabinets are closed every day.

Develop a schedule for monthly and quarterly checks. Check your first-aid kit once a month to make sure that it is fully stocked. Hold a fire drill once a month as well. Review your family contact information every several months to make sure that it is up-to-date.

Some things only need to be checked once! Conduct a thorough safety check when you first open your home for family child care. For example, verify that your home does not have lead-based paint or radon, that radiator and hot water pipes are insulated, and that heaters or furnaces are enclosed by barricades. Many of these safety concerns will be part of your licensing inspection. When you purchase new equipment, such as a crib, changing table, or safety gate, make sure that it meets Consumer Product Safety Commission standards.

Setting Up Your Home to Encourage Positive Behavior

Children respond best to environments that make them feel safe and secure. When they are given a special place to keep their belongings, children feel respected. When they know where to play, they are less likely to wander. When they know which things they may play with and which are off-limits, they learn to respect the rights of others. Children who have a wide variety of interesting and age-appropriate toys are more likely to become involved in purposeful play. When the environment supports group living, fights are rare and the day goes well.

When the environment is set up poorly, children may be confused. They may fight over toys or cry because they want a toy that another child is using. While there are many possible reasons for children's unwanted behavior, it's always a good idea to check the physical environment first to see if it is contributing to the problem. Here are some examples:

Unwanted Behavior	Possible Cause	How to Change the Environment
The children run around the home from room to room.	All of the rooms are interconnected.	Restructure the space by making one of the rooms out-of-bounds, by moving a piece of furniture in front of a pass-through, or by boxing in a play area with furnishings.

Unwanted Behavior	Possible Cause	How to Change the Environment
Children run without a purpose when they are inside.	There is no indoor area for active play and gross-motor activities.	Provide space for active play, such as dancing to music, rolling on rugs, or jumping on mattresses that are placed on the floor.
Children do not take care of materials or put them away.	Toys and materials are not organized in containers and are not placed where children can find and return them.	Store materials on low shelves that children can reach. Place toys with small pieces in dishpans or other containers. Label the shelves and containers so children know where to find and replace materials. Make a job chart to help children approach caring for FCC materials and furniture as a shared responsibility.
Infants, toddlers, and older children interfere with each other's activities.	Younger children do not have a safe space for crawling or toddling; older children do not have areas large enough for moving freely.	Set up safe, protected spaces where young infants can have tummy time and where mobile infants can crawl and walk. Include low tables where preschool children can play without being interrupted.
Children cry or fight a lot.	Children may be overstimulated by always being in a group or by having too many choices.	Have a quiet, cozy place for a child to spend some time alone, with one other child, or with an adult.

Organizing and Displaying Materials

Whichever approach you adopt for your FCC home, you will need low shelves to store toys and materials, and child-sized tables and chairs. Here are some additional guidelines:

Select well-made materials that are sturdy enough to last a long time.

Provide open-ended toys that children of different ages can use in different ways. For example, babies and 4-year-olds can both enjoy nesting cubes, baby dolls, and plastic measuring cups. Remember that, in addition to purchasing equipment and materials, you may be able to borrow some items from a toy-lending library in your community. Families may be able to donate some items, and you can collect or make many things. See chapters 10–20 for specific suggestions about appropriate materials for each age-group.

Supplement purchased toys and games with common household objects. Children delight in banging on empty coffee cans or oatmeal containers. Keep safety in mind when selecting and displaying materials, especially if you care for children of several ages.

Work with children's families and therapists to make sure that children with disabilities have toys and materials that they can use by themselves and with other children. For example, chubby, flat crayons and puzzles with knobs can be used easily by most children, including those with fine-motor limitations. A communication board or electronic device can help a child with a language delay communicate with friends.

When materials are organized and displayed thoughtfully, children are more likely to use and care for them. Storing materials so children can see and reach them helps children become independent because they can select and return materials by themselves. When materials are stored in an orderly, uncluttered way, children can find what they need and learn to take care of them. Low bookcases or plastic milk crates make excellent storage places. You can turn a closet into a storage space by installing shelves. Materials can be organized in cans, shoe boxes, and dishpans.

Here are some additional guidelines for organizing and displaying toys and materials:

Display a few carefully selected toys so children can see what is available and choose what they want to use.

Use picture and word labels on containers and shelves. Labels show that everything has a place. They help children find what they want and later participate in cleanup. Make labels by using photographs, drawings, or catalog pictures. Print the words, using lowercase letters unless the product name is written in uppercase letters (for example, LEGOS®).

Store toys and related materials where they will be used most often and group materials that are used together. Display them neatly on low shelves, making sure that children can only reach materials that are safe for them to use. Consider where to store materials that only school-age children use, materials that younger children use only with supervision, materials for adult use, and materials with small parts that are a choking hazard for infants and toddlers.

Provide duplicates of favorite toys. Young children often want to play with the same toys as their friends, but they are not yet ready to take turns or share. Having duplicates of favorite items helps minimize disagreements and waiting time.

Rotate materials regularly. As children outgrow or lose interest in toys that have been displayed, exchange them for materials that have been stored away.

Include materials that show a variety of cultural and ethnic backgrounds in positive ways, especially, but not only, those of the families in your program.

Here are some creative ideas that family child care providers have used for storage:

- Ice cream barrels can be used to store children's personal belongings. Add coat hooks on the wall over these containers.
- Stack wooden or plastic food crates, and glue or bolt them together. Paint them and use them as storage shelves.
- Add casters to an empty crate and use it as a movable trunk for dress-up clothes.
- Collect shoe boxes to store scissors, crayons, paper scraps, and puzzles. Be sure to label each box as described above.
- Keep toys with small pieces, such as table blocks, pegs, and figurines, in baskets or plastic containers.
- Store sensory materials, such as sand and rice, in covered containers.

Planning Your Day

Setting up for family child care means both arranging the physical space in your home and organizing your day. Having a consistent but flexible daily schedule, planning ahead, and preparing for the more hectic times of day can make your program go more smoothly.

Daily Events

Daily events in a family child care home include the routines of the day: hellos and good-byes, mealtimes, diapering and toileting, and sleeping and resting. They also include the experiences you offer each day. There will be times when you gather all of the children in your group for a meeting or read-aloud session, and times when you set up a small-group activity. There will also be choice times when children are free to choose where, with what, and with whom to play. You will also have outdoor play whenever weather conditions are not extreme. Of course, every day also includes transitions, the times when children change what they are doing. This section describes the events of the day and offers strategies for promoting children's development and learning during each.

Arrival

Children arrive at different times, and you may be caring for your own children as well as getting school-age children (both yours and FCC children) to the bus or school.

Plan something interesting for children to do independently. Books, story tapes, CDs, and table toys are good choices for the early part of the day. Children can use them in the kitchen while others are having breakfast. Some FCC providers have special "hello" toys that they make available only at this time of day.

Include children in setting up for breakfast. That will help make breakfast a relaxed, unrushed time.

Encourage children to begin choice time when they finish eating breakfast and have cleaned up their places at the table. They do not need to wait until everyone has finished before they help clean up and decide what to do.

Make sure school-age children have everything they need to start their school day.

Use arrival time as a learning time. Having a sign-in sheet or creating a "Who's Missing?" chart helps children learn to recognize their names and build other literacy skills.

Group Times

At times throughout the day, you may want to gather all of the children in your group together for a meeting or read-aloud time. For instance, at the beginning of the day, you may have a morning meeting, which some providers call a *circle*. During the meeting, you can greet each other, introduce new materials, sing, recite a fingerplay, talk about what you will be doing during the day, and help children transition to choice time. Here are some strategies for successful large-group times:

Plan ahead. Think about your purpose in order to make the most of group times.

Make group times interactive and engaging.

Keep large-group times short. At the beginning of the year, group times might be for only a few minutes. They may get longer as children get older. Take cues from the children as you decide whether to shorten or lengthen group times. Be ready to stop when children begin to lose interest. An infant may be happy to sit on your lap or play nearby during a group time. Allow toddlers to come and go (and maybe come back again). You may see them watching and listening as they play nearby.

Choice Time

During choice time, children choose what they would like to do, with whom to play, and what materials to use. Choice time is the most important teaching and learning time of the day. It typically lasts for an hour or more, not counting time to clean up. Children may choose blocks, toys and games, dramatic play, art, sand and water, stories and books, and so on. (See chapters 10–20.) When children are finished with one experience, they choose another. While all children will not usually be doing the same thing during choice time, you might plan a small-group activity, such as a cooking project in which children take turns participating. You can also conduct a planned literacy or math activity geared to children of a particular age. While children are engaged, you observe them, talk with them about what they are doing, ask open-ended questions, and make suggestions that extend their play and support learning. Here are some strategies for promoting children's development and learning during choice time:

Plan choice time. Use the information about children's interests and skills that you gain by observing them. Think about how choice time experiences help children learn concepts and skills in literacy, math, science, social studies, technology, and the arts.

Help children learn to make choices. During your morning meeting, talk about what you and the children will be doing during choice time that day. A chart with pictures can help children make choices. Give each child his or her name card to place on the chart to show where he or she will play.

Allow enough time. Meaningful learning cannot be rushed. A longer choice time lets children become engrossed in what they are doing. They engage in more complex play.

Interact with children during choice time. Talk to children about what they are doing. Ask open-ended questions to extend their play and learning and to help them talk about their ideas and feelings.

Add new materials, equipment, and props as children's skills and interests change.

Cleanup Time

Cleaning up can be challenging. When children are interested in their play, it can be hard for them to stop what they are doing to start something new. Use these strategies to help cleanup go more smoothly:

Handle cleanup playfully. Make it fun. Adapt a song and sing, "This is the way we wash the paintbrushes, wash the paintbrushes, wash the paintbrushes." Play cleanup games. For example, you might invite one child to put away all of the long rectangular blocks while another puts away all of the cylinders.

Remember that cleaning up is a learning experience for children. They learn math as they match blocks to the shapes outlined on the block shelf labels, and they use literacy skills as they look at the word and picture labels on the various containers for toys and other materials. Cleanup also promotes self-regulation. Children learn to stop one activity and begin another.

Give children a warning. Let them know that in a few minutes they will have to stop and clean up. You may want to use a special song or another signal that a transition is coming.

Label the environment so that children know where materials belong.

Remind children to clean up as they finish using materials. Encourage them to put materials away before they move on to a new experience.

Help children understand that cleaning up is everyone's job. Members of a community help each other.

Going Outdoors

Going outdoors involves a lot of details and two transitional times: going out and coming back in. Before you go out, coats, hats, snowsuits, and mittens go on. When you come in, they come off again. Bathroom breaks are a must before and after outdoor time. Here are some strategies to help these transitions go more smoothly:

Store children's clothing near the door and within their reach. Provide coat hooks, cubbies, and storage containers for items that children can put on by themselves.

Encourage older children to help the younger children with their buttons, zippers, or mittens.

Have extra hats, scarves, and mittens available for children who do not have their own.

Help children stay engaged once they have on their outerwear. Invite children to sing, do fingerplays, play simple games, or look at books while you help other children get dressed.

Minimize waiting time and do not expect children to line up to go outdoors.

Mid-Afternoon

If you have school-age children of your own or others in your care, the time at which they return from school can be very hectic. Other children may be waking up from their naps then, and they need your attention during the transition from nap time to snack time and afternoon experiences.

Have a snack ready so that both the children who are waking and the school-age children can help themselves. (School-age children may prefer to make their own snacks.)

Consider the individual needs and preferences of the school-age children and set up appropriate activities and choices for them. Some may want to do something very active after sitting for most of the day. Others may want to relax with a book or listen to music. Some may want to start their homework immediately, while others may want a break from academic work first.

Build in some individual time with your own children, especially if you have school-age children. Give them a chance to talk with you about their day.

End of the Day

Children are picked up at different times, and some will become anxious when they see other children leaving with their parents. Children, family members, and you are tired. You need to greet and exchange information with families while making sure that children are still engaged. Here are some end-of-the-day strategies that providers have found useful:

Plan some quiet activities for this time of day. Select toys and materials that can be put away easily, such as puzzles, table toys, crayons and paper, books, story tapes, and CDs. Some FCC providers offer special end-of-the-day toys the same way as they offer morning toys.

Spend a little time alone with each child, talking about the day and plans for the next day, reading a story, or playing together with one of the special toys. Some FCC providers help children dictate a letter to their families about what they did that day.

Schedule additional outdoor time at the end of the day.

Urge parents to try to keep a regular schedule so that their children and you can anticipate their pickup time.

Stay calm and help children stay calm if families are unavoidably late because of heavy traffic or an emergency.

Greet families as they arrive. Talk about their child's day and your plans for the next day. Find out about the family's plans for the evening. Send home a *LearningGames* activity or a book for the family and child to read together.

Transitions

Every day involves many transitions, the periods between one routine or experience and the next. Transitions can be difficult if children do not know what to do or if they have to wait long. Young children cannot wait happily. When they have to wait while adults get organized, disruptive behavior such as pushing and hitting often occurs.

Plan ahead. Think about what is coming next so you can give the children your full attention.

Be organized. Have supplies ready for the next experience so you do not have to search for them while children wait.

Give children a warning. Before a change takes place, tell the children that it is coming. For example, before cleaning up and washing hands for lunch, you might say, "It's almost time to clean up. Finish what you are doing, and then we'll help each other put the toys away. It's almost time for lunch."

Give clear directions. Make sure your instructions are appropriate for the developmental level of the child. For example, a child who can only follow one-step directions will be confused if, in one set of directions, you tell her to put the balls in the shed, go inside, hang up her coat, and wash her hands.

Avoid having children wait. Keep children engaged in an activity rather than have them wait. For example, if you're singing while children are putting on their coats, they can keep singing along as you help other children get ready. Some children may be looking at books while others are washing their hands for lunch. It is best not to have children sit at the table until lunch is ready.

Guide children through transitions. Do this by describing what you are doing and what children will do next. Some FCC providers have special songs for cleanup time and for getting ready for lunch. Make transitions fun by making them times for learning. For example, you can invite children to transition to choice time if their names start like *baby* or rhyme with *berry, cherry, merry, ferry*. Actively transition to the outdoors by having children hop like a bunny, lumber like an elephant, or trot like a horse as they go out.

Hectic Times

You may wish you could clone yourself for those times of day when you have to do several things at once. For example, as children arrive in the morning, you simultaneously greet them, exchange information with families, serve breakfast, and make sure that the other children are engaged in activities. At lunchtime, you may feed a baby, cook, supervise some children as they set the table, and watch others who are completing their morning activities. Perhaps you also recite a fingerplay or sing as children come to the table so they are engaged while you are putting out food.

Here are some ideas for making hectic times go more smoothly:

Imagine the day before the first family arrives at your door. Think about the children who will be there, the experiences you have planned, and the materials you will need.

Keep the daily schedule and routines as consistent as possible so children can predict what will happen and know what is expected of them.

Set a relaxed pace. Be flexible.

Invite children to share their skills as much as possible. Invite school-age children to read a story to the younger children while you set up an afternoon snack or encourage them to set up the snack while you read to the younger children.

Remember that perfection is not a realistic goal! Do not let stress prevent you from enjoying the children.

The Daily Schedule

A consistent daily schedule helps children learn the order of their day. Young children like to know that they can depend on daily routines. This helps them feel secure. When you say things like "We will play outside after your nap," children learn what to expect. The daily schedule also helps you organize your day and plan a good balance of routines and experiences for children. It also helps you balance active play and rest.

You may wonder how it is possible to establish a daily schedule when you care for children of varied ages and when each child has different strengths and needs. For example, infants need to eat, be changed, and sleep according to individual schedules. Toddlers and preschool children can play for longer periods of time, but they still need quiet times and naps. In fact, toddlers may need a morning and afternoon nap. School-age children come and go. They may be with you in the morning, go to school, and then return, sometimes full of energy but sometimes as tired as can be.

Here are some guidelines for developing a daily schedule:

Be aware of children's individual needs for sleeping, eating, and toileting. Follow an individual schedule for each infant in your group.

Include time for active play and quiet play.

Offer opportunities for children to play in small groups or by themselves, and time to interact just with you.

Plan at least an hour a day for choice-time experiences.

Allow enough time for unrushed daily routines.

Schedule time to go outdoors in the morning and afternoon. Allow 45–60 minutes for each outdoor period.

Plan for hectic times and transitions.

Try to schedule more challenging activities in the morning when children are most fresh.

If possible, schedule nap time directly after lunch. Children tend to be sleepy after eating.

Provide materials for children to use quietly after they nap. That way, tired children can continue to nap while those who are awake play with table toys or look at books.

The "Individual Care Plan" (ICP) forms you complete with the help of each family will also help you create your overall daily schedule (see chapter 5, "Partnering With Families"). The ICP forms give you information about when each child will arrive and go home (on most days), and when and how long each child naps or otherwise rests. For infants, the plan includes information about when the child eats, sleeps, and has his or her diaper changed. Once you have completed an "Individual Care Plan" form for each child, you can develop an overall schedule for your group that shows the approximate times of daily routines for each child. The actual times may vary from day to day, but a general schedule for routines will help you plan your day. For instance, it will help you avoid planning outdoor time when two infants are sleeping. Post the daily schedule so families can see it and know what to expect.

Sample Daily Schedule

Many factors influence your daily schedule. What time does your program open? When do families arrive? What time do school-age children leave for school? How old are the children in the group? Do you provide meals, or do families send food? What time do school-age children return? What are families' work schedules? How late are you open? Do you provide care around the clock?

The following chart gives suggestions for each daily event, including the approximate amount of time to allow for each. Your schedule will vary according to the needs of the children in your care, but the guidelines will help you think about your day.

Daily Event	What Happens
Early morning and arrival	As FCC children arrive, you get your own children up and ready for the day. You prepare and serve breakfast. Children wash their hands and eat breakfast as they arrive. After breakfast, you check and change infants' diapers and put infants down to nap on their individual schedules. The children help clean up after breakfast and play with table toys, read books, listen to story tapes or work at the computer until breakfast is over. School-age children leave for school.
Morning circle (15 minutes)	Read a story. Recite fingerplays or sing. Talk about plans for the day. Introduce new materials or concepts. Keep circle time short. Stop if you see that children are losing interest and are ready to be more active.
Morning choice time and snack (1 hour)	Toddlers and preschool children choose an experience, such as art, toys and games, dramatic play, sand and water, blocks, or stories and books. As they finish one experience, they move to another. Some infants and toddlers nap during this time. As infants wake up, you bring them to join the other children's play experiences or put them in a safe place to explore. Some providers offer a special project or work on a study with preschool children during choice time. They also offer small-group literacy and math activities several times a week for preschool children. Choice time ends with cleanup, and then snack time follows. Sometimes snack is served family style. The children wash their hands, help prepare the snack, and enjoy the food together with you. Some providers set up a snack bar so children can help themselves to a snack as they finish cleaning up.
Outdoor play (1 hour)	Children get ready to go outside. They use the toilet, wash their hands, have their diapers changed, put on outerwear, and so on. Outdoors, children play in your yard or at a nearby playground.
Transition indoors and to group read-aloud time (1/2 hour)	Children come inside, use the bathroom, and wash hands, or they have their diapers checked and changed. Children participate actively in a short read-aloud time. They continue looking at books or do other quiet activities as you prepare lunch.

Daily Event	What Happens
Lunch (30–45 minutes)	Wash hands. Involve children in setting the table and serving food. Sit with the children and eat family style. Bring infants' high chairs to the table so they can be part of the social experience. Children help clean up after lunch.
Nap time and afternoon snack (1–2 hours)	Everyone (except perhaps a baby who just woke up) has a rest period. Children transition to nap time by using the toilet; washing their hands; brushing their teeth; and going to their cots, mats, or beds. Preschool children who cannot sleep rest quietly and look at books. After resting or playing quietly for 30–40 minutes, they get up and begin a quiet activity. As children wake up, they use the toilet and wash their hands. Infants' diapers are checked and changed. Children eat a snack when they wake up. School-age children arrive and help themselves to a snack. Everyone cleans up from snack and chooses an afternoon activity.
Afternoon choice time and outdoor play (2 hours)	This is time for active indoor and outdoor play for all children, including school-age children. Some FCC providers take children outdoors right after nap time and then come indoors for afternoon experiences. Other providers schedule indoor experiences after nap time and go out in the late afternoon. Some offer a special project or work on a study.
Transition and afternoon meeting (1/2 hour)	Children either clean up from choice time or transition back indoors. Many providers have a short group time to talk about the day, make plans for the next day, read a story, and sing a good-bye song.
End of the day	Children go home at different times. They stay engaged in activities such as drawing, looking at books, or playing with table toys until their families arrive.

Display a word and picture schedule at children's eye level so they can learn the order of the day. An example is provided on page 48.

Children need a daily schedule that is regular enough to be predictable but flexible enough to meet their individual needs and interests and to take advantage of unexpected opportunities that arise during the day. Although you follow your schedule in a general way, you will want to use it flexibly. On a beautiful summer day, stay outside longer and have a picnic lunch outdoors. Invite all of the children to join a group movement experience, following a child's lead as she whirls around to lively music. Take advantage of unplanned events that present learning opportunities. A sudden thunderstorm, the mail carrier at the door with a package, or the discovery of a caterpillar in your play yard may interest the children and change your plans and schedule for the day.

Remember, too, that every infant has an individual schedule for eating, sleeping, diapering, and playing. Each infant is fed when hungry, sleeps in a familiar place when tired, and has his or her diaper changed when it is wet or soiled.

Planning Your Week

Weekly planning includes both planning for individual children and planning for your whole group. Taking each child's individual strengths, needs, and interests into consideration as you plan is called *individualizing* care and teaching. With its small group size, family child care provides an ideal setting for individualizing your program.

To plan purposefully, you need to observe children carefully, think about what you learn about each child, and use what you know about their interests and skills. As (or very soon after) you observe children during daily routines and experiences, you write brief notes about what they do and say. Here are some examples of questions to guide your observations:

- What materials does the child use?
- How does the child use the materials?
- How long does the child stay engaged in the experience?
- Does the child play with other children or alone?
- What do you notice about his or her social–emotional skills? Physical development? Cognitive and language skills?
- What literacy and math skills are emerging?

When you collect this information, you can use it to offer play experiences that address each child's developmental levels and interests. If you see that a child is fascinated by different sounds during a musical experience, you can provide homemade musical instruments so that the child can experiment with making musical sounds. To help a child develop fine-motor skills, you can plan experiences such as cutting paper, sifting sand, or playing with lacing and zipping boards. By knowing each child's levels in different developmental areas, you can build on and extend each child's skills.

To help you prepare for each day and respond to children's changing interests and skills, *The Creative Curriculum for Family Child Care* includes two weekly planning forms: the "Child Planning Form" and the "Group Planning Form."

The "Child Planning Form"

The "Child Planning Form" is used on a weekly basis to record current information about each child. It helps you use what you know about each child to plan experiences that support his or her development and learning. Each week, take a few minutes to review your observation notes; examine portfolio samples; and think about recent events, interactions, and conversations with families. Record the most important facts in the "Current Information" section. Then note how you will use this information in the coming week. For example, describe changes you might make to routines and list materials you might introduce to the child.

The following example of a partial form shows current information and plans for two of the family child care children profiled in this book.

Child Planning Form

Week of: __5-3-2009__

Child: Jeremy (8 months)	Child: Tamika (19 months)
Current information:	Current information:
At breakfast, Jeremy has been picking up pieces of cereal one by one. Karen mentioned that she is going to start using a sippy cup with Jeremy soon, although she's not planning to wean him completely from breast-feeding yet. This week Jeremy has been pushing up on his hands and knees. He looks like he's about to crawl. He squeals with delight every time he finds the rattle that I hide under a towel. We play that game repeatedly.	Tamika liked listening to and turning pages in *The Itsy-Bitsy Spider* board book. She started to try to do hand motions. At group time, she said, "Sing itsy spider." She played with the animal puzzle but needed a little help getting the pieces back into the right holes. She likes to play with containers in the kitchen while I'm getting lunch ready. She played with the big beach ball in the backyard.
Plans:	Plans:
Coordinate with Karen to add other finger foods for lunch and snack.	Continue rereading the book. Get out the spider puppet to use with the book. Do another simple fingerplay (maybe "Two Little Birds"). Clap while I sing. Look for other songs and fingerplays that have book versions. Put out some more simple puzzles. Let her play with containers and lids in the kitchen.
Play a game where he hands me a clutch ball and I give it back to him.	
Put a toy a little out of his reach and encourage him to crawl to it.	
Play toy-hiding games and let Jeremy find them. Hide a toy behind my back and encourage him to creep or crawl to find it.	

The "Group Planning Form"

The "Group Planning Form" helps you think about all of the children in your group and decide what changes to make to the environment, daily schedule, and routines. It also helps you determine what activities to offer during the week. It gives you an overall sense of direction for the week and a list of the materials you want to use. To complete the "Group Planning Form," think about the following questions:

- What interests the children now?
- What materials are the children using?
- What skills are the children developing?
- What is working well? What is not working well?

The following example of a completed form shows how to incorporate information from the "Child Planning Form" as you plan your week.

Group Planning Form

Week of: 5-3-2009

Changes to the Environment:

Add a clutch ball and a picture/word lotto game to the toys area.

Add spider puppet, song and fingerplay books, books with simple pictures, and books about exercise to the library area.

Add whistles and kazoos to the music and movement area; add feathers, cotton balls, and pinwheels to the toys and games area.

Set up obstacle course outdoors.

Bring out some simple exercise equipment (light weights, hula hoops, jump ropes).

Add birthday party prop box to the dramatic play area.

Changes to Routines and Schedule:

Add finger foods for Jeremy's meals and snacks.

Add 15 minutes to outdoor time for children to use the bubbles, pinwheels, obstacle course, and exercise props.

Family Involvement:

Coordinate Jeremy's new food with Karen.

Talk to Karen about coming next week to do yoga with the children.

Send home *LearningGames*:

    Jeremy—Game 32, "Sing Together"

    Jorge—Game 88, "In, Out, and Around"

    Nathan—Game 125, "Move and Say"

    Rosa Maria—Game 147, "Props for Pretending" (in Spanish and English)

    Keisha—Game 105, "Match and Name Pictures"

Group Planning Form, continued

Week of: **5-3-2009**

Events and Play Experiences

	Monday	Tuesday	Wednesday	Thursday	Friday
Morning meeting	Introduce large box; use positional words	Play with large box and use words *in, out, on, under, through, around*	Introduce kazoos.	Sing "Row, Row, Row Your Boat" with variations ("Blow, Blow, Blow Your Boat").	
Choice time	clutch ball game, picture lotto, large box in block area, birthday party prop box →		*The Itsy-Bitsy Spider* in library with felt board and finger puppet; kazoos in music area	Add blowing races in the water table. →	
Outdoor time	obstacle course with positional words; bubbles →		Play with exercise props and feathers →		Play with exercise props; blow like the wind and like the wolf in *The Three Little Pigs.*
Read-aloud time	Read and move to "Head, Shoulders, Knees, and Toes."	Read *The Itsy-Bitsy Spider* and demonstrate movements.	Read *Wiggle.* Have children perform the actions.	Read "Row, Row, Row Your Boat" and demonstrate movements.	Read *The Three Little Pigs* and have children pretend to blow the house down.
Special activities	Play blowing games with cotton balls, pinwheels, etc. →		Marching band with instruments that children can blow	Ariel's visit	Play Ariel's new blowing game with small groups of children

Notes: Check with Jorge frequently to see if he needs to use the toilet. Have Nathan blow the toy sailboat across the water table. Continue to describe Nathan's actions and encourage his use of words. Buy pinwheels. Explore whether the children are interested in exercise as a study topic.

Thoughts for Next Week: Add *The Three Little Pigs* felt board pieces to the library.

Allowing Flexibility

Although you develop a plan for each day, be ready to set your plan aside to address children's needs and to support their interests. If your plans are flexible and you feel free to revise them as often as you think best, you are more likely to take advantage of unexpected learning opportunities that arise during the course of each day. Remember that being responsive is more important than sticking to a plan. Always keep in mind that your positive interactions with children are more important than particular activities. Here are some suggestions for adapting your plans in response to children's needs and interests:

Think about the day before the children arrive. Review your weekly planning forms. Try to imagine how all parts of the day will fit together.

Assess the realities of the day. Will an infant need extra time and attention because she is teething? Did a family bring a bag of fresh apples, tempting you to make applesauce for snack? Is a sudden downpour making you cancel the walk you planned?

Remain flexible and adapt your plans as necessary. No matter how carefully you prepare, you must always be ready to change your plans. Perhaps the children will be frightened by an ambulance siren or excited by a helicopter overhead.

Be responsive to individual children's needs and interests. For example, if you know that Tyrone is studying recycling in school, you might consider doing a study about trash and garbage. If Keisha loves to cook and has been sequencing the parts of stories by using felt pieces in the library area, you might help her follow a word and picture recipe.

Plan for bad weather and poor air quality. Even when conditions are too extreme for the children to go outdoors, they still need to move. Find ways to encourage indoor movement on those days. (Do not forget that going outdoors in the snow or a little rain can be fun!)

Expect the unexpected. Backup plans will also help you get through the day when you have to clean up after a sick child or your own child is home sick.

Taking Care of Yourself

Being a family child care provider is both demanding and rewarding work. You work a long, long day. You're awake, thinking about and getting ready for the day long before the first child arrives. When the FCC children leave at the end of the day, you still have family responsibilities. You cook dinner, help your own children with homework, spend time with your spouse and other adults, and find a little time to review how the family child care day went and think about your plans for the following day. Remember to take care of yourself and your family. Only by taking care of yourself will you have the resources and energy to care for the children and families in your program.

Summary

Organizing your home for family child care includes setting up your physical space, structuring your day, and planning for each day and week. The challenge of integrating your job as a family child care provider with your role as a family member is addressed throughout this chapter and discussed further in chapter 4, "Caring and Teaching."

---

[1] National Association for Family Child Care. (2006). *Safety standards for NAFCC accreditation.* Salt Lake City, UT: Author.

Additional Resources:

National Association for Family Child Care. (2006). *Equipment standards for NAFCC accreditation.* Salt Lake City, UT: Author.

Modigliani, K., & Moore, E. (2005). *Many right ways: Designing your home child care environment.* Columbia, MD: The Enterprise Foundation.

3

What Children Are Learning

What Children Are Learning

When you work with children under age 5, you witness more learning and development than anyone will observe during any other period of their lives. What and how children learn during this period become the building blocks for school readiness. For older children who spend time with you, learning does not stop when they leave school each day. Just watch a school-age child experiment to see what a caterpillar likes to eat!

Providers who know what kinds of experiences to offer children at each stage of development are able to help children build a strong foundation for lifelong learning. Physical development and aspects of social–emotional, cognitive, and language development are addressed in chapter 1. This chapter will help you understand how to support learning in the content areas. It has six sections. At the end of each you will find the objectives for development and learning that relate to the topic of that section.

Nurturing a Positive Approach to Learning discusses social–emotional characteristics and dispositions that influence children's success as learners.

Building Language and Literacy Skills describes how children acquire communication skills. It talks about how they learn to hear, understand, and produce the sounds and rhythms of language; engage with books and stories; and learn about print concepts, cues for reading, letters, and writing.

Discovering Mathematical Relationships discusses children's beginning understandings about numbers and operations, geometry, measurement, patterns, and collecting and organizing information.

Exploring Like Scientists explains that young children are scientists who are curious about the physical and natural world around them. They are eager to find answers to questions, try their ideas, observe what happens, and make discoveries.

Learning About People is social studies: where and how people live, how they get along with others, how they solve problems, and how they lived in the past.

Creating Through the Arts explains that dance, music, drama, and the visual arts are media through which children can express their ideas and feelings. They also learn to appreciate the artistic expressions of others.

Integrating Learning Through Studies describes how you can lead children in studying a topic of interest by helping them raise questions and conduct firsthand investigations.

Nurturing a Positive Approach to Learning

Children who have strong social–emotional skills and a positive attitude toward learning enter school ready and motivated to learn. The ways children feel about themselves and they ways they relate to others influence what and how they learn.

For young children, learning depends on the trusting relationships they build with the important adults in their lives. The research on relationships, especially the importance of secure attachments, finds that young children develop strong social–emotional skills when their needs are met consistently by trusted adults and when they have positive interactions. Children who know that they are safe, loved, and cared for are eager to venture out to explore everything around them. When adults encourage these explorations and share children's excitement about new discoveries, children gain confidence in themselves as learners. This research is explained in greater detail in the "Applying Research and Theory to Practice" section of this book.

ZERO TO THREE, a nonprofit organization that works on behalf of very young children and families, identifies seven social–emotional characteristics that are essential for school readiness. These traits are more fundamental to children's school readiness than knowing letters and numbers. Here are ZERO TO THREE's definitions of the characteristics:[1]

> *confidence*—a sense of control and mastery of one's body, behavior, and world; the child's sense that he is more likely than not to succeed at what he undertakes and that adults will be helpful
>
> *curiosity*—the sense that finding out about things is positive and leads to pleasure
>
> *intentionality*—the wish and capacity to have an impact, and to act upon that with persistence
>
> *self-control*—the ability to modulate and control one's own actions in age-appropriate ways; a sense of inner control
>
> *relatedness*—the ability to engage with others based on the sense of being understood by and understanding others
>
> *capacity to communicate*—the wish and ability to verbally exchange ideas, feelings, and concepts with others
>
> *cooperativeness*—the ability to balance one's own needs with those of others in a group activity

As you observe the children in your family child care program, notice how they demonstrate these characteristics. Encourage their efforts and keep the characteristics in mind as you plan ways to support their development and learning. Here are general examples of what you would expect to see each child doing in ways that are appropriate for his or her age:

confidence—the child tries new things; shows pleasure when he or she makes a discovery or completes a task; asks for help when needed; uses words like *my* or asserts, "I can do it."

curiosity—the child explores and investigates objects and materials by using all senses; notices new things in the environment; asks questions about what, why, when, where, and how things happen

intentionality—the child chooses what to play with, has ideas about how to use things, stays with an activity for a period of time, tries different ways to solve a problem

self-control—the child responds to redirection, increasingly behaves in ways that are expected by adults, uses words to express feelings

relatedness—the child trusts familiar adults and has secure attachments, enjoys playing games such as peek-a-boo, takes an interest in what other children are doing, is increasingly aware of the emotions of others, enjoys playing with other children, makes and keeps friends

capacity to communicate—the child uses vocal sounds, gestures, facial expressions, and eventually words or signs to express ideas and feelings, ask and answer questions, and have conversations

cooperativeness—the child imitates others and participates in small-group activities, begins to follow simple rules, helps put away toys or wipe a table, contributes ideas, and respects the ideas and efforts of others

The children in your family child care home will be more likely to develop these seven characteristics when you show them every day that you genuinely care about them. Talk with them in calm and respectful ways, take joy in their discoveries, have appropriate expectations about what they can do, and guide their behavior in positive ways. Every interaction you have with a child is an opportunity to nurture a positive approach to learning and to build a strong foundation for skills in literacy, mathematics, science, social studies, and the arts.

Objective for Positive Approaches

Objective 11. Demonstrates positive approaches to learning

Building Language and Literacy Skills

Children begin developing language and literacy skills as soon as they are born. When responsive adults talk with them, engage them in conversations, read to them every day, and teach them songs and rhymes, children are eager to communicate in all of the ways that you do: talking, listening, reading, and writing.

In your family child care home, children need many experiences that enable them to acquire vocabulary and other language skills, including discriminating the sounds of language; enjoying books and stories; and exploring cues for reading, print concepts, letters, and writing.

Vocabulary and Language

One of the greatest achievements in the first few years of life is the development of oral language. This includes the ability to understand the words that they hear (receptive language) and to put their own ideas and feelings into words so they can share them with others (expressive language). A child with a good vocabulary and language skills can engage in conversations, share ideas and feelings, ask and answer questions, and work through problems.

Research shows that children who have large vocabularies and who use verbal language to communicate tend to become good readers and are more successful in school.[2] Reading, after all, is figuring out the meaning of printed text. The more words a child knows, the more he understands when someone reads to him and when he later learns to read, himself. School-age children continue to build their vocabularies in the various subjects they study in- and outside of school, especially when adults talk with them about what they are learning.

Children communicate in a variety of ways. In addition to spoken words, they use other vocal sounds, approximation of words, facial expressions, gestures, and signs. If you care for children whose primary language is not English, you should encourage them to continue using their home languages as they also learn English. Dual-language learners are more likely to become better readers and writers of English if they also understand the words and ideas in their home languages.

Children show you in many ways that you are helping them develop vocabulary and other language skills.[3]

An infant might

- say, "Ma-ma," and "Da-da"
- understand some words (for example, wave her hands when you say, "Bye-bye," or point to a ball when you ask, "Where's the ball?")
- string sounds together and repeat the sounds in a sing-song voice that begins to sound like speech (for example, "Ba-ba-*ba-ba-ba*-ba-ba-ba")
- respond when you ask a simple question (for example, point to her nose when you prompt, "Show me your nose.")

- use 10–50 single words that refer to people, objects, and events, simplifying some words (for example, *ba* for *bottle* or *ma* for *more*)
- communicate with signs or pictures if he or she is unable to speak

A toddler or 2-year-old might

- combine words into two-word sentences (for example, "Daddy car," or "More milk.")
- use a questioning intonation to ask questions (for example, "What dat?" or "Go out?" or "Where mommy?")
- use signs or pictures in a sequence to express an idea (for example, *baby + cry*)
- begin to use language to get information by asking *who, where, what,* and *why* questions (for example, "Why you going?" or "What this?" or "Where teddy?")
- begin to use prepositions (for example, *in, on*); pronouns (for example, *me, he, we*); negatives (for example, *cannot, do not)*; and conjunctions (for example, *and, but, or*)
- understand and follow simple directions and stories

A preschool child might

- ask you the meaning of a word he or she does not know
- describe the details of an experience (for example, "I went fishing with my dad, and we caught a big fish. My mommy cooked it up, and we ate it. It was good!")
- use new words in conversation (for example, call a scary dream a *nightmare* after hearing you read the book, *There's a Nightmare in My Closet*)
- explain the meaning of a word (for example, "That means mix together" when you ask whether anyone knows what the word *combine* means)

A school-age child might

- ask you for a dictionary to look up an unfamiliar word in a book he or she is reading
- give a lengthy description of something that happened at school
- recognize when he makes a verbal mistake and correct himself (for example, "That was funny! I said 'speronsible,' but I meant 'responsible.'")
- show you a list of new words she has to learn for homework and ask for your help

What You Can Do and Say

- Talk to children about what you are doing during routines: "I'm going to change your diaper now. You will feel much better when we're finished. First I'm going to…"

- Describe what a child is doing: "You like those nesting cups, don't you? You like banging them together. Now you're banging them on the floor. Look! You tried to put one inside the other, and it fit!"

- Expand on what a child says: When he says, "Go out," you can say, "Do you want to go outside to play?" If she says, "More milk," you can say, "You finished all of your milk. You must have been thirsty. Now you want more milk. Here it is."

- Ask open-ended questions to encourage children to verbalize their ideas.

- Listen carefully and wait patiently as children express themselves. Do not rush them.

- Label storage containers and shelves with pictures and words.

- Introduce new words: "That big machine is called a *front-end loader.*" "This book is called, *The Enormous Turnip.* Can you think of something else that is *enormous?*"

- Offer a dictionary and help a child look up the meaning of a word.

Language Sounds (Phonological Awareness)

The ability to hear and distinguish the sounds and rhythms of language is another important literacy skill. *Sound awareness,* the ability to notice and distinguish different sounds, is the first step in developing phonological awareness. Even newborns have the ability to distinguish their mother's and father's voices from other voices or noises they hear around them. You may have noticed that a baby pays particular attention to the type of speech called *parentese.* When you speak slowly in a high-pitched, sing-song voice, face-to-face with an infant, he is likely to pay attention to you long before he understands what you are saying. You may feel a bit silly talking this way, but it is very effective in getting infants to listen to your voice.

During the preschool years, most children develop *phonological awareness,* the ability to hear the small units of sound in spoken language. They notice rhyming words in songs, poems, fingerplays, and stories. They enjoy playing with words, such as saying *Banana-fana-fo-fana.* Preschoolers begin to hear and clap the syllables in their names, for example, Sam·an·da and Ty·rone. They also notice that some words start with the same sound, such as *cat* and *cake,* or *Denise* and *Danny.* Once they become readers, school-age children use what they know about letter sounds and other cues to figure out words they do not recognize.

Everyday experiences help children learn about the sounds and rhythms of language and eventually to distinguish among language sounds. Here are examples of what you will observe:

An infant might

- put sounds together ("da-da-da"), listen intently when you imitate them, and then repeat the sounds again and again
- calm when she hears you sing the same lullaby she hears at home
- string sounds together in a sing-song voice
- anticipate the part of a song during which you do something interesting (for example, "Trot, trot to Boston. Trot, trot to Lynn. Watch out, Jeremy! Don't fall...*in*!")
- attempt to voice sounds of animals and things (for example, "baa-baa"; "choo-choo")

A toddler or 2-year-old might

- fill in the rhyming word in a predictable refrain when you pause before saying the word
- recognize familiar environmental sounds (for example, a fire truck siren, a chirping bird, a car horn, and the ring of a phone)
- play with the sounds of familiar words (for example, "Nanabana")
- repeat words he or she enjoys hearing and saying (for example, "Pop, pop, pop")

A preschool child might

- join in saying and singing rhymes, poems, and songs
- make up nonsense or silly names (for example, *Silly Willy* or *Funny Bunny*)
- clap each of the syllables in a name (for example, Jer·e·my and Tan·ya)
- notice that some names start with the same sound (for example, *Jonelle, Juwan,* and *Jerome*)

A school-age child might

- sound out a written word she does not recognize and sometimes ask you for help
- explore rhymes (for example, say, "I need a word that rhymes with *flower* for my poem.")

What You Can Do and Say

- Recite nursery rhymes, clapping along with the beat: "Patty cake, patty cake, baker's man. Bake me a cake as fast as you can."

- Talk about animal sounds: "What does a cow say? 'Moo.' What does a dog sound like? 'Woof-woof.'"

- Sing songs that encourage children to listen for and anticipate actions: "Ring around the rosie...Ashes, ashes, we all fall down!" or "Open, shut them...give a little clap."

- Read stories with rhymes and lots of repetition, such as *Is Your Mama a Llama?*, *The Bear Snores On*, and books by Dr. Seuss.

- Call attention to similarities of words: "*Tanya* and *Timmy* both start with the same sound: /t/. Can you think of another word that starts with the /t/ sound?"

- Help a child sound out an unfamiliar word as he or she is reading.

Stories and Books

Reading books and sharing your pleasure in language and stories are among the most important ways you can help children become readers. Children who regularly hear stories read aloud develop a foundation for literacy, including the motivation to learn to read. Most children who enjoy being read to develop a love for books that will last throughout their lives, enriching their experiences and stretching their imaginations.

As you share books and stories with young children, you will be rewarded by how much they are learning from their experiences.[4]

An infant might

- snuggle into your lap and watch intently as you turn each page

- turn pages and play with the moving parts of a book (for example, tabs to open or pull)

- point correctly to the picture of a familiar object when you ask where it is (for example, "Where's the dog?" "Can you show me the baby's eyes?")

- shake his head when you read the word *no* (for example, when you read a book like *Is Your Mama a Lama?* and you say, "No-o-o. My mama's a ...")

A toddler or 2-year-old might

- make the sounds you have modeled as animal speech or other environmental sounds (for example, "Moo, moo" or "Choo, choo") in response to pictures or something you read
- pretend to read the story, talking as if she were reading the text
- make connections between the content of a story and what he sees around him (for example, get a toy truck after seeing a picture of one in a book)
- protest when you misread a familiar word or leave out a word
- ask you to read a favorite book repeatedly

A preschool child might

- anticipate and recite refrains in a familiar book
- listen to a story and ask questions or comment about it
- make up stories with a beginning, a middle, and an end
- select books to look at and read independently
- use books to find answers to questions (for example, to identify a caterpillar found in the yard)
- act out a familiar story

A school-age child might

- seek a quiet place to read a book after school
- read a story to younger children and act out the parts
- use books to do research for homework
- enjoy having you read a chapter book to him

What You Can Do and Say

- Provide cloth, soft plastic, and cardboard books that infants can grasp, chew, and manipulate; simple picture and story books for toddlers and twos; and both story and content books for preschoolers and school-age children. Display them where children can reach them.

- Hold children on your lap or close to you as you read. Talk about the pictures and story.

- Encourage children to chime in as you read a predictable book and to help you tell the story of a picture book without text.

- Ask questions as you read a story to preschoolers: "What do you think will happen next?" and "Did that ever happen to you?"

- Discuss books that school-age children are reading to find out what topics they are thinking about and what their ideas are.

Letters, Print Concepts, and Writing

Reading and writing go together. A group of letters is a symbol for a word, just as letters are symbols for sounds. Long before children can recognize letters and read or write letters and words, they begin to understand that one thing can represent something else. For example, a picture of a banana represents a real banana, a block can stand for a car, and logos mean a company name or a product.

Children are inspired to write if they often see print, hear it read aloud, and see you writing for different reasons. They develop literacy skills when you encourage them to explore writing and when you talk with them learn about letters and print concepts.

An infant might

- watch you as you write a note
- make random marks on paper with large crayons

A toddler or 2-year-old might

- draw horizontal and some vertical lines and make circular marks
- experiment to see what kinds of marks she can make: lines, dots, zigzags
- begin to recognize common logos and some letters, especially the first letter of his name
- write lines and other marks that begin to look like letters

A preschool child might

- scribble across a piece of paper, include some letters, and then read aloud what she wrote
- write a sign for a building he made with blocks
- look at an alphabet chart and tell you which letters are in her name
- write his name, using an initial capital and writing the rest of the letters in lowercase
- identify a letter by its name as you read a book together (for example, say, "That is a *w*," and point to the first letter of each word in the phrase "Wishy-washy, wishy-washy")
- arrange the magnetic letters on your refrigerator to spell her name

A school-age child might

- write a book review for a homework assignment
- use the computer to write a social studies report
- write a preschool child's description of his picture
- make signs or write plays
- keep a journal

What You Can Do and Say

- Point out environmental print, such as letters on alphabet blocks, on children's clothing, or in displays.
- Use picture and word labels on containers for toys and materials.
- Provide large crayons, water-based markers, paint and brushes, and large chalk for toddlers and twos. Offer plenty of plain paper so they can use these tools to make marks, scribble, paint, and write.
- Display the alphabet in different ways: magnetic letters, a chart, alphabet books, and puzzles with letter pieces.
- Encourage older children to write and use the computer for research and word processing.

Objectives for Language and Literacy

Objective 8. Listens to and understands increasingly complex language

Objective 9. Uses spoken language to express thoughts and needs

Objective 10. Uses appropriate conversational and other communication skills

Objective 15. Demonstrates phonological awareness

Objective 16. Demonstrates knowledge of the alphabet

Objective 17. Demonstrates knowledge of print and its uses

Objective 18. Comprehends and responds to books and other texts

Objective 19. Demonstrates emergent writing skills

Incorporating Language and Literacy in Daily Experiences

The chart below gives examples of ways to enhance the experiences you provide for children by including materials that promote language and literacy learning.

Blocks	Dramatic Play	Toys & Games
Provide paper, markers, and tape for children to make signs for buildings.	Offer books and magazines for children to use while playing house.	Talk about colors, shapes, and pictures in a lotto game.
At the children's eye level, hang charts, artwork with captions, and photos that show environmental print.	Introduce a variety of purposes for print (e.g., recipes, shopping lists, receipts, greetings, etc.).	Provide matching games to promote children's visual discrimination skills.

Art	Sand & Water	Library
Invite children to dictate stories to go with their artwork.	Add literacy props to the sand area, such as letter-shaped molds and toy road signs.	Offer an assortment of recommended children's books.
Share books about famous artists and their work.	Encourage children to describe how the sand and water feel.	Set up a writing area with pens, markers, pencils, paper, rubber stamps, ink pads, envelopes, etc.

Discovery	Music & Movement	Cooking
Offer books about scientific topics (e.g., insects, plants, seeds, etc.).	Write the lyrics of a favorite song on chart paper.	Make recipe cards with pictures and words.
Provide paper and markers for children to record their observations.	Encourage children to use instruments for sound effects as you tell stories together.	Talk about words and letters on the food containers.

Computers	Outdoors
Write and illustrate the steps for using a computer.	Bring colored chalk and other writing materials outside.
Use a drawing or simple word-processing program to make a book with children.	Have children examine street signs in the neighborhood.

Discovering Mathematical Relationships

Mathematical thinking involves noticing similarities and differences; organizing information; and understanding quantity, numbers, patterns, relative position, and shapes. Learning the concepts and language of math—*more, fewer, smaller, the same as, how many*—gives children a sense of order, a way to make predictions and comparisons, and ways to solve problems.

Children discover mathematical relationships every day when they explore space, compare amounts, and sort and match objects. As Jean Piaget explained, young children need many opportunities to explore and manipulate interesting objects. Lev Vygotsky emphasized the important role of adults who take an interest in what children are doing and who talk with children about their discoveries.[5]

To promote children's mathematical thinking, it helps to know which math concepts are basic and what experiences are appropriate. While it may have been a long time since you studied math, you can provide experiences to help children explore numbers and operations, geometry and spatial sense, measurement, patterns, and collecting and organizing information.[6]

Number and Operations

This aspect of mathematical thinking involves learning about and using numbers. Numbers and operations include

- counting (numbering items in a particular order)
- matching the appropriate number with each of the items being counted (one-to-one correspondence)
- figuring out how many objects are in a group
- comparing groups and figuring out which groups have more and which have fewer
- understanding rank order (first, second, third, last)
- recognizing numerals
- putting groups of objects together to find out "how many in all"

- making equal groups
- understanding that fractions are parts of wholes (for example, halves, thirds, and fourths)

You help children understand number concepts when you use numbers in everyday activities, sing songs that include numbers, invite children to help you set the table, and provide materials for them to explore.

An infant might

- look at you intently as you put on her socks and you say, "Here's one sock for this foot and one sock for your other foot. Two feet; two socks."
- smile when you bring more cereal and ask, "Do you want *more* cereal? You must be hungry!"
- place a lid on each plastic container
- reach for more objects with which to play
- make a sign for "more" after finishing a cracker

A toddler or 2-year-old might

- stomp around the room, singing, "One, two, one, two, five."
- put a cup on each plate or a napkin on each placemat on the lunch table
- notice that another child has a larger lump of dough and ask you for more
- line up a set of cars and place one block next to each car
- build a tower with blocks and announce, "Mine bigger."
- hold up two fingers and say, "I two," when you ask, "How old are you?"

A preschool child might

- notice that it takes five scoops of sand to fill a cup
- try to count 10 blocks but not match every number with a block
- respond, "I'm four," and show you four fingers when you ask how old he is
- organize a collection of bottle caps by color and say, "There are more white ones."
- stand by the door to go outside and say to a friend, "I'm first, so you can be second."

A school-age child might

- use numbers to identify quantities, for example, count 10 plastic bears and write the numeral *10*
- figure out how to distribute 15 marbles to three children so each has the same number of marbles

- keep score in a card game
- know that half of an apple is more than a fourth of an apple

What You Can Do and Say

- Sing songs and fingerplays that include numbers, for example, "One, two, three, four, five. I caught a fish alive." Recite nursery rhymes that mention numbers, such as "One, Two, Buckle My Shoe."
- Count with children, touching each object as you count: "Let's see how many trucks we have. One, two, three, four. We have four trucks."
- Provide toys that engage children in exploring size, such as nesting cups and stacking rings.
- Use comparison words: "You picked out the *heaviest* rock." "You're telling me that you want a *smaller* ball."
- Use words that indicate order: "Who wants to be *first* to stir the pancake batter? Who wants to be *second*?"
- Encourage children to compare quantities: "Do we have more red playdough or more green playdough?"
- Use numbers as you talk with children about what they are doing: "You had two apple slices, but you ate one. Now you have one slice left." "You have three markers, and I have three. We have the same number of markers."
- With preschool children, play board games that involve counting, such as CHUTES AND LADDERS® and CANDYLAND®, and play simple card games that promote numeral recognition, such as "Go Fish."
- Provide more complex board games for school-age children. Have them keep score during games for which that is appropriate.

Geometry (Shapes and Space)

Geometry involves recognizing shapes, size, position in space, direction, and movement. An understanding of geometry and spatial sense begins with recognizing similar shapes and understanding body positions in space. Children gain spatial sense as they become aware of themselves in relation to objects and people around them. They learn about location and relative position (for example, on, off, under, below, in, out, near, far, next to). Eventually, these skills and concepts lead to an understanding of geographic mapping.

An infant might

- place his hands around a bottle, feeling its shape
- experience being wrapped in a blanket
- run her hands back and forth along the edge of a table

- crawl through a tunnel, enjoying the feeling of being in an enclosed place where she can see out
- bang blocks against different slots in a shape-sorting box until they fall through
- drop a ball into a basket

A toddler or 2-year-old might

- try to put a teddy bear into a box that is too small; then find a larger box and put the bear into it
- play with various shapes and put all the cubes in a bucket
- decide whether to go around or through a structure in order to get an object
- learn the names of some shapes (for example, explain, "This is a circle. Like a pizza.")
- bend down to look when you say, "Your shoes are under the table."

A preschool child might

- say, "You put your horse inside the fence. I'm going to make mine jump over the fence."
- note that a sandwich is a rectangle
- say, "I made a square," after putting two triangular blocks together
- show his friend how to build a block boat and tell him, "Do it this way. You need a square block like this. You have to turn it up to make it fit."
- use empty boxes and tubes to build a doll playground

A school-age child might

- explore ways to fill an area (for example, use pattern blocks and put 5 diamonds or 10 triangles inside the outline of a flower)
- classify shapes by attributes (for example, explain that squares, other rectangles, and diamonds are all four-sided shapes)
- use geometric language to describe shapes and spaces (for example, "A rectangle has four lines and four angles.")
- build shapes by using other shapes (for example, use two small tangram triangles to build a parallelogram, a square, and a larger triangle)

What You Can Do and Say

- Play body games such as pat-a-cake and "This Little Piggy."

- Provide large cardboard boxes and tunnels that children can use to experience different positions in space and the words that indicate them, for example, *inside, outside, over, under,* and *next to.*

- Use positional words: "Let's put all the balls *in* the box." "Keisha is sitting *next to* Tyrone." "Here comes your shirt, *over* your head. Now your arm goes *in* the sleeve."

- Include materials and toys with different shapes and talk about what they are called.

- Help children explore the attributes of shapes by encouraging them to cut food into various shapes, such as cutting toast into triangles and squares. Have a theme for the day; for example, serve circular foods like crackers, cucumber slices, and tortillas.

- Offer school-age children geoboards, tangrams, pattern blocks, and computer programs that involve drawing shapes and manipulating them.

Measurement

Measuring involves such skills as figuring out how long or short something is or how much something weighs. When young children say things like "I'm bigger than you" or "This rock is heavy. I can't move it," they are using the language of comparison and measurement. They may begin measuring with nonstandard tools, such as a piece of string or their feet, before they use a ruler or tape measure.

Knowing about measurement includes

- describing how long or tall something is, how much a container holds, how heavy an object is, how much space is covered, and much time a task takes

- comparing two objects by particular attributes (characteristics); comparing three or more objects or events and putting them in order

- choosing a useful tool to measure something

As infants, toddlers, and twos examine, play with, and compare toys and objects, their explorations lay the foundation for learning about measurement. By the time they are preschoolers, children begin to be interested in measuring things.

A preschool child might

- count how many cups of sand it takes to fill a bucket
- use a piece of ribbon to measure the length of a book
- walk heel–toe across a room to figure out how many "feet" long the room is
- tell another child, "I'm more than you. I'm four and a half!"
- ask, "When will we eat the cookies?" when she hears the oven timer buzz

A school-age child might

- use a ruler to measure earthworms he found in the garden and determine which is the longest
- ask you for a scale to see how much she weighs
- use a tape measure to determine how long a piece of wood needs to be for a project

What You Can Do and Say

- Use measurement words and talk about relative amounts: "You are getting so *heavy,* I can hardly pick you up!" "This red sock is *longer* than the blue one." "This leaf is big, but that one is even *bigger.*"
- Encourage children to compare: "Are you trying to figure out who is *taller*? Stand back-to-back so we can compare."
- Invite children to estimate things like how many cups will fill the bowl or how many steps it takes to walk across the living room.
- Make picture and word recipes for children to follow. Show how many cups, tablespoons, teaspoons, and so on are needed for each ingredient.
- Provide standard measuring tools for older children to use, such as scales, rulers, yardsticks, measuring tapes, clocks, timers, and measuring cups.

Patterns

Patterns are formed when objects, events, or sounds are repeated a number of times in a particular order. The ability to figure out a pattern involves recognizing the relationships among its parts. For example, there might be a pattern of sizes, such as large, small; large, small; large, small; and so on. There are color patterns, such as red, blue; red, blue; red, blue; and so on. When daily schedules are consistent, children also begin to understand the pattern of daily events: "After my cereal, I get a bottle."

To begin to develop the ability to recognize, continue, or create patterns, young children first need many opportunities to explore and manipulate objects, notice their similarities and differences, and describe their relationships.

An infant might

- stroke a rough carpet and feel a smooth tile floor
- play with nesting cups, trying different sizes until she finds one that fits inside another
- place several small blocks in a line, scatter them around the floor, and then collect and line them up again

A toddler or 2-year-old might

- use a small cup to fill a larger one with sand
- say a repetitive phrase from a story book while you read it aloud
- point to the Papa Bear in a book when you ask, "Which bear is bigger?"
- line up cars of different sizes, grouping the big ones together and the little ones together
- group all the green pegs together and the red pegs together in a pegboard
- place the graduated rings of a stacking toy in correct order so they all fit on the post

A preschool child might

- line up small cars in a pattern of red, black; red, black; red, black, and so on
- make up a movement pattern like stomp, clap, clap; stomp, clap, clap; and so on, and ask you to follow it
- point out a snake's pattern of white, brown; white, brown; white, brown; and so on in a picture
- sponge paint a patterned border around a drawing
- create a pattern with interlocking cubes

A school-age child might

- describe a pattern made with blocks: "Red, blue, yellow; red, blue, yellow; red, blue, yellow…"
- continue counting by fives after you prompt, "Five, ten, fifteen…"
- order a group of objects according to size, quantity, texture, or weight (for example, put a collection of balls in order from largest to smallest)
- recognize a pattern in a pattern block design and be able to continue it

What You Can Do and Say

- Sing repetitive songs, follow consistent routines, and talk about events of the day: "First we put away the toys. Then we can go outside. When we come in, we'll read a story."

- Read books with predictable language, for example, *Brown Bear, Brown Bear, What Do You See?*.

- Point out patterns so children become aware of them. "Look at the stripes on your shirt: a red stripe, and then a yellow one. Red, and then yellow again." "You lined up the cars: a big car, then a little one, a big one, and then a little one."

- Provide toys that children can use to make patterns, such as colored wooden blocks, large beads and laces, and pegboards with large pegs. Also offer common objects, such as plastic spoons and forks, bottle caps, buttons, and keys, for children to use for patterns.

- Make a pattern and have children see if they can keep it going. Ask a child to make up a pattern for you to copy.

- Help school-age children notice more complex patterns, for example, on a number chart. Continue a pattern that repeats some units and grows, for example, one, two, one, three, one four, one, five, and so on.

Collecting and Organizing Information

We think mathematically whenever we organize information in a logical way in order to make comparisons. When babies begin to notice that some things are the same and some are different, they are beginning to sort and classify. Preschoolers might make a collection of leaves, sort them into piles according to type, and organize them on a three-dimensional graph to compare how many they have of each type. School-age children are able to conduct surveys and make graphs to show the results. They organize collections into categories and count the number in each set, and they roll dice, make predictions about which sums will occur most often, and record their findings.

Collecting and organizing information includes

- recognizing how objects are the same and different
- separating objects into groups by features such as size, color, shape, sound, and use
- presenting information by using objects, drawings, pictures, charts, and graphs
- describing information by using words like *more, fewer, the same number as, smaller than,* and *not* (for example, "The shapes in this group are circles. The shapes in that group are *not* circles.")

An infant might

- recognize your voice and stop crying when he hears you say, "I know you are hungry. I am coming right now with your bottle."
- distinguish between familiar and unfamiliar adults
- show a preference for a particular blanket and enjoy stroking it
- hit a xylophone with a stick but shake a rattle
- pick out all the banana slices from a fruit salad
- collect wooden blocks and put them in a box

A toddler or 2-year-old might

- see a picture of a donkey and say, "Horsie"
- place a blue block next to another blue block
- place blocks of various shapes into the matching opening in the shape-sorter box
- put all of the yellow blocks in a bucket
- pick out all of the round beads from a pile of assorted beads
- select all of the cubic blocks from a pile of different shapes and then build a tower

A preschool child might

- sort a collection of bottle caps into two groups: grooved caps and smooth caps
- explain how she organized the toy cars (for example, "The red cars are here, the blues ones here, and the green ones are here.")
- draw a picture of each object that floats and each that sinks after testing them in a tub of water
- graph a sticker collection, sorting them by type and showing quantities and relative amounts

A school-age child might

- sort by several attributes (for example, gather a set of large red plastic circles)
- use a tally system to find out what ice-cream flavor people prefer: chocolate or vanilla
- observe the weather and collect data about the number of rainy days during a particular period
- predict an outcome and test the prediction (for example, predict which sum of two faces will occur most frequently and then roll two dice 50 times)

What You Can Do and Say

- Provide toys young children can fit together (for example, containers with matching lids or objects that fit into muffin tins).

- Display toys on shelves and in containers labeled with a picture and word and explain how you organized them and why.

- Point out how children organize things: "You put all the red pegs in a row"; "You lined up all the blue cars."

- Provide collections that children can organize in different ways, such as large plastic bottle caps, plastic animals, and shells. If the children are old enough to use small items, have them sort the items in egg cartons so they can line up the groups and compare the amounts.

- Offer school-age children graph paper to keep track of data and make comparisons. Also encourage them to make predictions, for example, ask, "When you flip a coin 20 times, how many times will it land heads-up?"

Objectives for Mathematics

Objective 13. Classifies and sorts

Objective 14. Uses symbols and images to represent something not present

Objective 20. Uses number concepts and operations

Objective 21. Explores and describes spatial relationships and shapes

Objective 22. Compares and measures

Objective 23. Demonstrates knowledge of patterns

Incorporating Mathematics in Daily Experiences

Blocks	Dramatic Play	Toys & Games
Suggest cleanup activities that involve sorting by shape and size.	Add telephones, menus, and other items with numerals on them.	Provide collections for sorting, classifying, and graphing.
Use terms of comparison when you talk with children about blocks (e.g., *taller*, *shorter*, and *same*).	As you participate in the children's play, talk about prices, addresses, and times of day.	Have children extend patterns with colored cubes, beads, etc.

Art	Sand & Water	Library
Use terms of comparison, e.g., "That piece of yarn is longer than your arm." Provide empty containers of various shapes for creating structures.	Provide measuring cups and spoons, and containers of various sizes. Ask estimation questions (e.g., "How many cups will it take to fill the container?").	Add numeral stamps to the writing area. Include books about math concepts (e.g., size, number, comparisons, shapes, etc.).

Discovery	Music & Movement	Cooking
Offer tools for measuring and graphing. Provide boxes and materials for sorting by size, color, and shape.	Play percussion games that emphasize patterns (e.g., soft, loud, loud; soft, loud, loud; etc.). Use language that indicates spatial relationships (e.g., *under, over, around, through*).	Use a timer for cooking. Provide measuring cups and spoons.

Computers	Outdoors
Include software that focuses on number concepts, patterning, measurement, shapes, etc. Offer a drawing program that children can use to create patterns.	Have children look for natural patterns. Invite children to collect items during a walk and then sort, classify, and graph the items.

Exploring Like Scientists

Science is way of searching for explanations and understandings about the physical and natural world. It involves finding answers to interesting questions: What does this feel like? How does this work? Why did this happen? What would happen if we tried it another way? How can we make this work better?

Scientists are curious and eager investigators. They wonder about what they see, try their ideas, observe what happens, and draw conclusions. A new discovery often leads them to investigate more. Opportunities to explore and investigate are everywhere for those who are interested.

Young children are born scientists. They are curious about everything and want to figure out how things work. They believe there is a reason for everything, and they ask endless *what*, *where*, *why*, and *how* questions: What makes thunder? Where do the fish go when the lake freezes? Why are the leaves orange now? How can a snake move if it doesn't have legs? How does a caterpillar turn into a butterfly?

You don't have to be a scientist, yourself, to be an effective science teacher for young children. Science is all around you. You can take advantage of daily routines and everyday experiences indoors and outdoors to encourage children's curiosity and desire to investigate the world round them. Young children can explore three aspects of science: the physical world, life science, and Earth and the environment.

The Physical World

Physical science involves exploring the physical properties of objects and materials. Young children gather information about the physical world by using all of their senses. What does that feel like? Is it slimy, squishy, hard, or sticky? How does it smell? Is it loud or quiet? Is it fast or slow? How can I make it move? Can I roll it, twist it, blow on it, or push it? What will happen if I drop it on the floor? Older children have ideas and test them. They may build a ramp to race cars and see how far they will go, predict which objects will sink or float, and pick up objects with a magnet.

Throughout the day, you will see children touching, tasting, smelling, listening to, looking at, manipulating, and experimenting with objects to learn about the physical world around them.

An infant might

- mouth and then shake a rattle you place in her hand
- raise his bottle and continue sucking when the milk level drops
- pull aside a blanket you used to hide a toy (understand object permanence)
- repeatedly drop objects on the floor to see what happens
- push the buttons on a pop-up toy to make various items appear; then push the items down and start again
- watch you make a soft toy squeak; then squeeze it to reproduce the sound

A toddler or 2-year-old might

- push a chair across the room and stand on it to reach a toy
- experiment to see what sounds he can make with a xylophone and with bells
- try using different tools at the water table (for example, watering cans, cups of different sizes, funnels, scoops, sponges, basters)
- use a plastic screwdriver and hammer to turn bolts and pound pegs on a toy workbench
- use words to describe the properties of objects (for example, *hard*, *smooth*, *heavy*, *sticky*)

A preschooler might

- say, "Look! My red paint ran into the yellow paint, and they made orange!"
- test different kinds of balls to see which bounces highest and which rolls farthest
- roll a toy truck down a ramp; then tilt the ramp to make the truck roll faster and further
- use a balance scale to weigh rocks and see which are heaviest
- sort a collection of buttons
- take apart an old clock to see how it works

A school-age child might

- notice that materials can be changed from one state to another: solid, liquid, and gas (for example, observe frozen and boiling water, or cook an egg and see that it changes from a liquid to a solid)
- discover that her hands become warmer when she rubs them together very fast
- experiment with the variety of sounds that can be produced by putting different amounts of water in bottles and striking them gently with a spoon
- test objects to see which ones a magnet will pick up and figure out what else the objects have in common

What You Can Do and Say

- Place objects in infants' hands that they can hold, manipulate, and mouth safely.
- Give a baby a spoon to hold while you feed her with another spoon. Explain, "You can hold a spoon and help feed yourself."
- Offer a basket with colorful fabric scraps of different textures for children to examine.
- Provide collections of objects for children to explore and play with, such as large plastic bottle caps, plastic containers, and balls.
- Show interest in children's discoveries: "That dough feels soft and squishy, doesn't it?" "You figured out how to make music with those bells. You just shake, shake, shake them."
- Provide magnets, magnifying glasses, and containers so children can collect and examine objects.

Life Science

Life science is learning about living things. Young children are fascinated by people, animals, and plants. They want to answer many questions: What does the rabbit like to eat? How loud can I make my voice? What will happen if I pick this flower? Where did all these leaves come from? Which animals lay eggs? What do animals and plants need to grow? How does my body work? What is a life cycle?

An infant might

- discover her toes, grab her feet, and try to put them into her mouth
- touch your mouth as you sing
- play with your hair as you hold him
- watch a fish in a bowl
- look into a tree when she hears birds chirping
- play with the grass and dandelions in the yard
- enjoy the sound of crunching leaves as he crawls on the playground

A toddler or 2-year-old might

- get excited when he sees a squirrel scamper across the yard and up a tree
- collect acorns and watch them roll down the slide again and again
- pretend that a doll is a baby and take her for a walk in a stroller
- fill a pail with damp sand, pat it down, and turn it upside down to make a pretend cake
- watch a line of ants march along the sidewalk and try to figure out where they are going
- ask you, "Where snow go?" when she sees that the snowman she helped build the day before is no longer there
- help you water the plants in the garden
- hold a carrot for the pet rabbit to eat and say, "He hungry."

A preschooler might

- use a magnifying glass as she counts a beetle's legs
- wonder, "Do fish ever sleep? Do they drink the water?"
- plant seeds, water them, and track their growth
- look in a book to learn about earthworms
- compare different kinds of leaves to see how they are the same and different

A school-age child might

- do research to learn about the habits and needs of a pet in order to care for it
- keep a journal of the life cycle of a caterpillar or mealworm
- help you plant a garden, weed it, and keep it watered
- collect insects from the garden, examine them with a magnifying glass, and look them up on the Internet to find out what they are and what they do
- look in a book to identify various birds that he sees in the neighborhood

What You Can Do and Say

- Provide natural materials for children to explore and examine, for example, shells, feathers, and flowers.
- Offer containers so children can collect things like seeds and leaves.
- Plant a small garden outdoors or have indoor plants for which children can help care.
- Place a covered fish tank where children can watch the fish, or let them help take care of a pet like a hamster or guinea pig.
- Talk with children about how to stay healthy.

Earth and the Environment

For children, this aspect of scientific study involves learning about the immediate environment, including natural materials like rocks, sand, and dirt, and about less concrete things like weather, seasons, the moon, and the stars. Your location will influence the kinds of experiences you can provide for children to explore the Earth and the environment. Even very young babies take an interest in their immediate environments.

An infant might

- notice moving shadows on the wall or a curtain blown by the wind
- reach toward falling leaves
- pat the water in a puddle

A toddler or 2-year-old might

- collect sticks in the backyard, put them in a bucket, and then play with them
- pick up a small rock, place it on the slide, watch it roll down, run after it, and then repeat the same actions many times
- fill a bucket with snow, bring it inside, and then wonder why the snow disappears and the bucket has water

A preschooler might

- examine a prism and see that colors appear on the wall when he turns it
- create shadows by using a flashlight and various objects
- collect vegetable and fruit scraps to put in the compost pile
- wonder why the moon is not always round
- help track the weather on a calendar and compare the number of sunny, cloudy, and rainy days each month

A school-age child might

- check the weather forecast on the Internet and report it to you
- bring a newspaper story about a tornado and talk to you about what happened and how to stay safe
- suggest that you set up a recycling system
- notice what animals are doing to prepare for winter
- identify the Big Dipper in the night sky

What You Can Do and Say

- Take children outdoors each day to experience an environment that is entirely different from the inside of your home. Point out what you observe: "See how the wind is blowing the trees? Look, the clouds are moving, too!"
- Talk about the seasons and how the environment changes throughout the year: "I can tell that it is fall. The leaves are turning red, yellow, brown, and orange. Acorns are all over the ground."
- Create a large calendar on which children can keep track of the weather.
- Set up a compost system in the backyard and use the material in a garden.

Objectives for Science

Objective 24. Uses scientific inquiry skills

Objective 25. Demonstrates knowledge of the characteristics of living things

Objective 26. Demonstrates knowledge of the physical properties of objects and materials

Objective 27. Demonstrates knowledge of the Earth's environment

Objective 28. Uses tools and technology to perform tasks

Incorporating Science in Daily Experiences

Blocks	Dramatic Play	Toys & Games
Talk with children about height, length, width, weight, and balance. Encourage children to investigate momentum, velocity, and incline by experimenting with ramps, balls, and marbles.	Introduce props such as a stethoscope or binoculars. Model hygiene skills by washing dolls and toy dishes.	Talk about balance and weight as children use table blocks. Sort, classify, and graph natural items such as rocks, leaves, twigs, and shells.

Art	Sand & Water	Library
Describe the properties of materials, especially as they interact (e.g., *wet, dry, gooey, sticky*). Use water and brushes for outdoor painting so children can explore evaporation.	Make bubble solution and provide different kinds of bubble-making tools. Put out magnifying glasses and sifters so children can examine different kinds of sand. Provide a variety of objects for floating and sinking experiments.	Include books about pets, plants, bodies, water, inventions, etc.

Discovery	Music & Movement	Cooking
Include nontoxic plants that children can care for. Offer tools, such as a magnifying glass and a microscope, that children can use to observe the properties of objects.	Set out bottles with different amounts of water so children can investigate sounds by tapping the bottles. Record children's voices as they sing; play them back for children to identify.	Encourage children to taste, smell, touch, listen, and observe during each step of the cooking process. Discuss how heating and cooling change substances.

Computers	Outdoors
Have children observe cause and effect by hitting a key or dragging a mouse.	Take pictures of a tree or bush the children see every day and discuss how it changes during the year.
Explain what you are doing as you add or change computer components.	Have children listen to their heartbeats or feel their pulses before and after running or exercising.

Learning About People (Social Studies)

Social studies involve learning about people: where and how people live, work, get along with others, solve problems, and lived in the past, and how their lives are shaped by their surroundings. Even infants are social scientists; people are more fascinating to them than any toy or object. They recognize the sound of their parents' voices and can distinguish familiar people from strangers. Before long, they can identify the people in their families and people who belong to other families.

Every day in your program, children explore social studies topics. When you talk with them about what they see on a walk with you around the neighborhood, children begin to learn about geography. They notice how people are the same and different. They learn firsthand about responsible citizenship: to make choices, understand different points of view, resolve conflicts peacefully, and treat others respectfully. When you provide props for children to enact experiences at the grocery store or a clinic, they gain a better understanding of various jobs and how people do them. As they develop and learn, children look back on how they have changed and what has changed in their environment.

Social studies topics to be explored with children include

- places and geography
- people and how they live
- people and the past

Places and Geography

Geography for young children involves learning about the physical characteristics of the place in which they live. They also discover relationships among places they know well and places that are less familiar. They begin by exploring the environment around them and take an interest in getting from one place to another. A beginning understanding of mapping includes learning how to get to the bathroom and playground and learning which direction to walk on a trip to the store. That kind of learning is supported when children build roads and structures with blocks. Older children learn to make and read maps, understand that a globe represents the Earth, can identify continents and countries, and appreciate how physical conditions affect all aspects of life.

An infant, toddler, or 2-year-old might

- crawl, walk, climb, jump off, crawl through, and investigate spaces and structures in the environment
- begin to understand words that describe position (for example, *next to*, *on*, and *under*)
- point to an apartment building and exclaim, "Mine!"

A preschooler might

- say on a walk, "I know where the mailbox is. It's right around the corner."
- build a road with houses and a gas station and explain, "This is a city. The cars go here on the road. If they need gas, they come to the station, and I fill them up."
- look at a picture of a bridge and try to make one like it with blocks
- tell you, "We went on a plane to Mexico. It was far away. It was hot there, so we didn't need our jackets. We even went swimming!"
- look at a map with you and identify land, rivers, lakes, and oceans

A school-age child might

- understand that maps are representations of actual places
- draw a map of the neighborhood
- use a globe to find countries
- talk about how climate affects the way people live and what they do
- complete a puzzle of the United States and identify most of the states

What You Can Do and Say

- Take children on neighborhood walks and talk about what they see: "We're going to walk two blocks to the library. Let's notice what there is to see."
- Point out the physical characteristics of places you visit: "Look how tall the apartment buildings are on this block."
- Play board games like "CHUTES AND LADDERS™" with children as a way of introducing directionality, which is important for understanding maps.
- Create an obstacle course for children to follow outdoors.
- Offer older children maps and a globe and talk about various countries.
- Help school-age children find and use the online mapping games offered by National Geographic Society.

People and How They Live

This aspect of social studies includes people's physical characteristics; similarities and differences in their habits, homes, and work; different kinds of families and roles; how people relate to each other; and the jobs they do. The younger the children, the more focused they are on themselves and their own families.

An infant might

- get excited when she sees familiar people enter the room
- gaze at photographs of family members
- watch other babies with great interest
- point to himself in the mirror when you ask, "Where is the baby?"

A toddler or 2-year-old might

- act out family scenarios, such as feeding a baby, pushing a doll in a carriage, or talking on the phone
- understand the sequences of routines (for example, get his special blanket when you say it is nap time or go to wash hands when you announce that lunch is almost ready)
- pretend to be a firefighter when playing with a fire truck
- show an understanding of the rules (for example, say, "No!" instead of hitting a child who tries to take something from her)
- identify himself as a boy or herself as a girl

A preschooler might

- talk about family members
- describe his parents' jobs
- point out that he or she has the same hair color as another child
- use a toy cash register while pretending to sell shoes
- remind another child of the rules (for example, say, "You have to use the blocks on the floor, not on the table.")
- finish a bottle of water and tell you, "We need to recycle this."

A school-age child might

- talk about similarities and differences in family structures, lifestyles, customs, and habits
- recognize the basic needs of all people for food, water, clothing, shelter, and clean air; look at a book about different kinds of homes around the world
- describe how people depend on one another for goods and services (for example, explain, "The farmer sells his vegetables and milk. Then he has money to buy clothes and things."
- talk about the kinds of work people do and the skills and tools they need in order to perform their jobs
- identify the need for rules and insist that everyone follow them

What You Can Do and Say

- Keep photographs of children and their family members in an album so children can look at them.
- Take walks and talk about the different jobs of people in your neighborhood (for example, mail carrier, firefighter, store clerk, and librarian).
- Involve children in helping to develop rules about getting along and cooperating.
- Provide paint, crayons, and construction paper in various skin tones.
- Provide props and dress-up clothes so children can act out the roles of people they know.
- Discuss picture books that show the daily lives of people who live in different parts of the world.
- Read stories about people and familiar situations, and help children relate the stories to their own lives.

People and the Past

Learning how people lived in the past is history. Young children focus on the here and now. They do not have much understanding of the concept *long ago*. They learn about time in relationship to themselves, including their daily schedule, what they did yesterday, and what they will do tomorrow. Gradually they come to understand concepts about time and events that have already happened.

A preschooler might

- hold up a baby shoe and say, "My foot used to be this little. Now it's big!"
- say, "A long, long time ago, I went to my aunt's house and played with my cousins."
- use a sand timer to take turns
- say, "I'm going to finish this picture tomorrow."

A school-age child might

- enjoy reading stories about people who lived long ago and talk about the differences between their lives and people's lives today
- make a book about his life and family, beginning with his experiences as a baby
- interview grandparents about life when they were young and what they did differently from today

What You Can Do and Say

- Follow predictable routines and a consistent schedule so children learn that there is an order to each day. That helps them begin to develop understandings about time.
- Talk about events that children can recall: "Remember yesterday? It rained so hard, we couldn't go outside."
- Point out things that change in your neighborhood: "This used to be a small grocery store, but they made it much bigger."
- Invite grandparents to come to your program and talk about their lives as children.
- Use words like *today, tomorrow, yesterday, next week, before,* and *long ago* as you talk about events and routines.
- Have children bring in pictures of themselves as babies or an article of their baby clothing. Discuss how the children have changed over time.
- Ask children questions that help them recall events: "What did you do last time we had a big snow storm?"
- Offer school-age children stories about long-ago times and far-away places.

Objectives for Social Studies

Objective 29. Demonstrates knowledge about self

Objective 30. Shows basic understanding of people and how they live

Objective 31. Explores change related to familiar people or places

Objective 32. Demonstrates simple geographic knowledge

Incorporating Social Studies in Daily Experiences

Blocks	Dramatic Play	Toys & Games
Include figurines that represent persons who have various jobs and cultures. Display pictures of buildings in the neighborhood.	Include props related to different jobs and social roles. Add multicultural dolls and props such as cooking utensils, play foods, empty food containers, and clothing.	Select puzzles and other materials that show or are related to diverse backgrounds and jobs. Play board games that encourage cooperation, following rules, and taking turns.

Art	Sand & Water	Library
Include paint, crayons, markers, and construction paper of various skin tones. Encourage children to paint, draw, and write about what they saw on a field trip you took together.	Invite children to talk about roads and tunnels they make in sand. Hang pictures of bodies of water (rivers, oceans, lakes, ponds, and streams).	Include books that depict diverse cultures, genders, and persons of different abilities. Show children how to use nonfiction books, including picture dictionaries and encyclopedias.

Discovery	Music & Movement	Cooking
Set up a recycling area where children sort paper, cardboard, glass, metal, and plastic into bins.	Show videos that present the languages, music, and dances of many cultures. Include instruments from different cultures.	Encourage parents to bring in favorite recipes. Visit stores that sell foods of different cultures.

Computers	Outdoors	
Encourage children to work cooperatively with software that helps them research a study topic or represent their learning.	Take many trips in the neighborhood and talk about what you see.	
Develop rules with the children for using the computer. Post them in the area.	Invite children to make maps of outdoor environments by using chalk on concrete.	

Creating Through the Arts

The arts involve creating, designing, expressing, and exploring ideas and feelings by using a wide range of materials. Children mix paints; pound and shape playdough and clay; build structures with blocks, boxes, and construction toys; dance to music; dramatize stories; chant; and sing. The arts are a joyful part of their lives and another language with which to express themselves.

You will find many practical ideas for offering children enjoyable and meaningful experiences in movement, music, drama, and visual arts in other chapters. By offering children open-ended materials and encouraging them to use them freely, you convey that their ideas, feelings, and self-expression are important.

Movement

When children dance, they express feelings and ideas by moving their bodies in response to music. Most children are able to move easily; you only need to encourage and appreciate their enjoyment. As they get older, they may be a little more inhibited and may prefer to learn and follow a dance routine.

An infant, toddler, or 2-year-old might

- rock back and forth to music

- imitate your movements as you dance

- participate in a simple dance routine like "Hokey Pokey"

A preschool or school-age child might

- use scarves and streamers as he or she moves to music

- imitate animal movements after watching a video

- move quickly to a polka and slowly to a lullaby or spiritual

- create a dance routine and teach it to others

What You Can Do and Say

- Sing and play music as you hold an infant and dance around the room with a toddler.

- Teach simple dance routines such as "Head and Shoulders."

- Offer children scarves and streamers to use as they dance to music.

- Play different kinds of music that will inspire children to move quickly (polka), slowly (spiritual), or precisely (a march).

- Have children move as if they were large elephants, slithering snakes, hopping toads, or graceful birds.

- Have a school-age child teach younger children a popular dance routine.

Music

Music involves combining voices and/or instrumental sounds to create melodies and pleasing rhythms, or just listening to and enjoying different kinds of music. Music can affect both emotions and behavior. A lively melody can inspire children to get up and move around. A quiet, slow melody can calm children and help them relax.

An infant, toddler, or 2-year-old might

- relax against your shoulder as you sing a lullaby

- repeat "row, row, row" as you sing "Row, Row, Row Your Boat"

- beat a drum, trying to keep time with the music on a CD

- sing and hum parts of a familiar song as he finger paints

A preschool or school-age child might

- sing a song on her own

- make up new lyrics to a well-known song

- say, "That music makes me think of a parade."

- learn to play a simple song on a xylophone

- identify different instruments by sound (for example, a saxophone, a piano, a guitar)

- play an instrument and read music

What You Can Do and Say

- Record or learn lullabies that are familiar to infants and use them to comfort a child.

- Rock, pat, and move with children to the beat and melodies of different musical pieces.

- Provide safe musical toys the children can manipulate and control.

- Sing and teach children different kinds of songs: fingerplays, folk songs, singing games, story songs, songs about routines, and so on.

- Play different types of music and talk about the differences: classical, marches, folk, rap, etc.

- Set up an area where children can explore and play various instruments.

Drama

Drama involves telling stories through action, dialogue, or both. By acting out familiar stories and making up their own plays, children develop language skills and an understanding of story structure. They also learn to cooperate with others. Drama is a wonderful way for children to learn and have fun.

An infant, toddler, or 2-year-old might

- imitate your gestures as you sing "The Wheels on the Bus"

- hold and rock a baby doll

- crawl across the floor and bark like a dog

- pretend to talk on a toy phone

A preschool or school-age child might

- gather props and act out "Goldilocks and the Three Bears"

- make up and put on a puppet show

- say, "Let's pretend that…," and suggest ideas to encourage other children to join in

- write and direct a play, giving out parts and explaining what each person should do and say

What You Can Do and Say

- Play peek-a-boo and other social games with infants.
- Encourage children to imitate and pretend by playing with them.
- Provide props for dress-up and dramatic play and take on a pretend role, yourself.
- Have children act out a familiar story by serving as the narrator and helping children remember what different characters say.
- Provide puppets and props, and encourage children to put on a play.

Visual Arts

The visual arts include painting, drawing, making collages, sculpting clay or playdough, weaving and stitching, print making, and more. Children need opportunities to work with different kinds of paint and paper; draw with crayons; cut with scissors; mold dough; and clean up with mops, sponges, and brooms. They learn to use different kinds of materials to express their ideas and show what they know.

An infant, toddler, or 2-year-old might

- make crayon marks on a large sheet of paper
- enjoy the feel of finger paint
- roll playdough and pretend it is a snake
- use large chalk to draw on the sidewalk
- paste collage materials on construction paper

A preschool or school-age child might

- create a get-well card for a friend
- mix blue and yellow paint to make green paint
- draw a picture of the people in her family
- create a structure using "beautiful junk"
- paint a picture in the style of a famous artist
- create a torn-paper picture after looking at books illustrated by Leo Lionni

What You Can Do and Say

- Collect soft, textured fabrics and crinkled tissue paper for infants to explore.

- Offer toddlers and twos jumbo crayons; large colored chalk; stubby, short-handled brushes; paint; playdough; and finger paint.

- Provide open-ended materials older children may use for creations: markers, crayons, paper, paints, clay, paste and collage, playdough, utensils, glue, and scraps of wood and fabric.

- Talk about techniques for illustrating books, such as using torn paper, watercolors, pastels, and pencils.

- Encourage children to draw pictures to show what they have learned.

- Display children's work attractively and protect artwork children want to take home.

Objectives for the Arts

Objective 33. Explores the visual arts

Objective 34. Explores musical concepts and expression

Objective 35. Explores dance and movement concepts

Objective 36. Explores drama through actions and words

Incorporating the Arts into Daily Experiences

Blocks	Dramatic Play	Toys & Games
Encourage children to build simple scenery, such as a bridge for acting out *The Three Billy Goats Gruff.* Display posters that include geometric shapes and patterns.	Display fine art posters that inspire dramatic play. Provide props to help children explore different roles.	Include materials that have different art elements (e.g., games that involve patterns, textures, and colors). Add building toys (e.g., LEGO® pieces, a Tinkertoy® set, etc.).

Art	Sand & Water	Library
Provide a variety of media for children to explore, including clay, paint, collage, and construction materials. Invite a local artist to share his or her work.	Display photographs of sand sculptures and encourage children to sculpt sand. Offer tools for drawing in wet sand.	Talk about art techniques used by illustrators (e.g., Leo Lionni's torn-paper pictures). Include children's books about famous artwork.

Discovery	Music & Movement	Cooking
Provide kaleidoscopes and prisms and encourage children to draw the designs they see. Collect natural materials when you take neighborhood walks with the children. Encourage the children to use the materials for collages.	Provide a variety of musical instruments to explore. Add scarves, streamers, and costumes to encourage dancing.	Encourage children to be creative while preparing their snacks. Dramatize foods being cooked (e.g., a kernel of corn popping or cheese melting).

Computers	Outdoors
Include drawing and painting software. Include software that enables children to create music.	Bring art materials outdoors. Provide streamers and scarves for outdoor dance and movement activities.

Integrating Learning Through Studies

One interesting and exciting way to promote children's learning is through in-depth, long-term studies. This is sometimes called the *project approach*. Studies enable you to involve children of all ages (particularly those ages 3 and older) in a common effort. Together, children investigate a subject of interest to them, integrating content in meaningful ways.

Whether you call it a *study* or a *project*, this approach involves organizing learning experiences in a way that is both relevant and exciting for children. The strongest feature of a study is its support of children's curiosity, their desire to explore the world and make sense of their experiences.

Throughout a study, you can observe and record children's comments and questions, their involvement with materials, and their interactions with each other. To help you reflect on each child's development and learning, you can collect samples, photographs, and photocopies of their work. Remember to date each piece and write a short note about the context in which it was created.

Begin by selecting a topic that is appropriate for your group. Ideas may originate from any source—you, the children, or the children's families. *The Creative Curriculum Study Starters* provide step-by-step guidance for developing studies of 13 topics that children frequently find interesting. You might choose to develop a study around something that children have asked you about (for example, how their bodies change), a social concern (for example, food we eat), or an unexpected event (for example, ants in the kitchen). The best topics are relevant to children's experiences (topics that build on what children already know). The following questions can help you select a good topic:

- Can children explore the topic firsthand, in a variety of ways over an extended period? Can objects be manipulated? Can it be explored easily in your home?

- Are resources available, such as people to talk with, places to visit, objects or living things to observe and explore, and books to read? Can children do some research for this topic independently, without depending entirely on you?

- Will the topic permit children to learn literacy, math, science, social studies, the arts, and technology in real-life contexts?

- Will the children be able to represent their learning about the topic in a variety of ways (for example, through pretend play, by writing, and by making constructions)?

- Will family members want to get involved with the study? Is the topic respectful of cultural differences?

- Can the topic be explored by children of different ages?

As an example, the following scenario illustrates why you might conduct a study about trash, garbage, and recycling in your family child care home.

On a walk one day, the children in your FCC proram were fascinated by the garbage truck. They watched and listened as the truck stopped at each house along your street. They imitated the sound of the truck when it crushed the trash. When they came inside, they built houses in the block area and rolled toy trucks in front of them to pick up the garbage. They also brought the wastebaskets from various places in your family child care home into the dramatic play area to dump into a large box. On the next several neighborhood walks, they became aware of trash on the streets and soon expressed an interest in picking up litter along the route. Coincidentally, Tyrone's class at school began a recycling project. The students, who were learning about which items are recyclable, began collecting newspapers and plastic containers.

You realize that the children are really curious about trash and garbage. You review the guidelines to determine whether it would be a good study topic. After saying *yes* to each of the questions, you decide to build on the children's interest by engaging them in a study. Here is an explanation of how you might help children in your family child care home study trash, garbage, and recycling.

1. **Find out what children already know.** Observe children as they explore objects and pictures related to trash, garbage, and recycling. Listen to what they say. Then ask them, "What do you know about trash and garbage?" Record their answers on chart paper. Post the paper on the wall.

   Here are some examples of what children might say:

   - "Garbage is dirty and smelly."
   - "Some people throw their trash on the ground."
   - "Garbage can make you sick. My mother says not to pick it up."
   - "At my house, we recycle newspapers every week."
   - "In my house, the sink grinds up the food we don't eat. It makes a lot of noise."

2. **Learn what children want to find out.** During a group time, ask, "What do you want to find out about trash, garbage, and recycling?" Record the children's questions on chart paper and post the paper on a wall. Add to the list as the study progresses.

   Here are some examples of the questions children might ask:

   - "Who collects the garbage from our FCC home?"
   - "When is the garbage collected?"
   - "Where does the garbage truck take the garbage?"
   - "Why do we separate newspapers, glass, and plastic?"
   - "Why do we put some food in the compost bin?"
   - "Why do we put some food in the sink?"

3. **Think about what children can learn.** Consider how you will address literacy, math, science, technology, social studies, and the arts during this study. Here are some suggestions for a study of trash and garbage:

Literacy

- Keep lists of observations, discoveries, and new vocabulary related to trash and garbage.
- Read and discuss books about trash and garbage, such as *The Day the Trash Came Out to Play*; *The Garbage Truck; I Stink*; *Too Much Garbage*; *Recycle!: A Handbook for Kids*; and *Trash! Trash! Trash!*.
- Look for the recycling symbols on empty containers.
- Encourage children to draw, write, and talk about trash and garbage.
- Start a list of the kinds of litter children find, such as paper, plastic, and metal containers or other objects. Add to the list throughout the study.

Math

- Count, sort, categorize, and measure trash and garbage.
- Take a neighborhood walk and compare the shapes of different kinds of trash and garbage containers in the neighborhood.
- Use a stopwatch to see how long it takes each of several children to move a pile of newspapers into a wagon. Make a chart to compare the children's times.

Science and technology

- Encourage the children to examine and compare trash and garbage items by using their senses of touch, smell, sight, and hearing.
- Find out how garbage trucks and sink disposals work.
- Consult Web sites related to trash, garbage, and recycling.

Social studies

- On a trash-collection day in your neighborhood, take the children outdoors to observe the collection.
- Visit a recycling center or landfill.

- Involve children in picking up litter on neighborhood walks, in local playgrounds, or in other locations. (Provide gloves and bags and make sure that children don't pick up broken glass and other hazardous materials.)
- Interview the trash collector. Find out what he or she likes and does not like about the collection job.

The arts

- Ask families to save and send in newspapers, clean food containers, and other recyclable materials, and have children use throwaways for art projects.
- Reuse clean plastic spoons, foil pans, cardboard tubes, and cans to make musical instruments.

4. Add materials:

- blocks—toy garbage trucks and small containers to use as miniature trash cans
- dramatic play—props to create a recycling center
- toys and games—a bottle cap collection for matching and sorting, and a sanitation worker or garbage truck puzzle
- art—objects to recycle as collages and constructions, and newspapers for papier-mâché
- library—fiction and nonfiction about trash and garbage, and an audio recorder to use during interviews with sanitation workers
- discovery—old phones, clocks, and small appliances to take apart
- cooking—a container to collect garbage scraps to compost
- outdoors—trash collected on a neighborhood walk to use for sorting, counting, and predicting

5. Investigate the children's questions. Assign children to investigate particular research questions. Ask open-ended questions to encourage further discoveries. Observe how children are investigating, and suggest additional materials and resources. Decide whether to teach particular content material directly.

Here is a sample investigation:

Question: What do we throw away in our FCC home?

What To Do:

- Tell children that they are going to sort the trash in one of the trash containers in your FCC home to find out what kinds of things get thrown away. Give children rubber gloves to wear and tell them that it will be a safe task.
- As children take turns taking objects from the trash bag, help them categorize the items. They might sort the trash by its source, such as the kitchen or the art area, or they might sort it according to what it is made of, such as plastic, paper, metal, cloth, rubber, or wood.

– As they sort, place the items on large pieces of paper or cardboard. When the sorting is finished, write the names of the categories on each large background piece and have the children glue the items onto the paper or cardboard.Ask children what they discovered about trash by sorting it. They might notice the least and most common types of trash. They might notice some things that should not have been thrown away at all. They might be surprised at the quantity of trash. Record their discoveries on chart paper.

– Weigh the trash on the bathroom scale. Repeat the task on other days. Encourage children to predict how much the trash will weigh and then to check their predictions.

6. **Involve families.** Families may think that trash, garbage, and recycling is a strange topic, so it is important to help them understand why you selected this topic and how they can participate in this study at both FCC and home. You might wish to send a letter to families about the children's study of trash and garbage. Families can do many things at home with regard to this topic, from starting a compost heap to avoiding the purchase of overpackaged goods. This study can really benefit your community!

7. **Celebrate learning.** When you notice that children are losing interest, bring the study to a close. Plan a special way to celebrate the children's learning and accomplishments.

- Invite families to come for a festive cleanup day at a local park or recreation area. After picking up trash, have a trash-free picnic.

- Have a "beautiful junk" art show. Everything must be made from objects that would otherwise be put in the trash.

When you conduct studies with preschoolers and older children, simplify study-related experiences for **toddlers and twos**. Toddlers and twos can participate in a study if they are interested in the topic. Choose simple, appropriate experiences for them that relate to the topic.

- Go on a neighborhood walk to pick up trash. Give toddlers or twos a paper grocery bag and help them collect items during the walk. When you get back home, talk about what they found.

- Let toddlers and twos help you empty the FCC trash containers on trash day and put the containers out for the trash and recycling collectors.

- Go outdoors when the trash collectors come and watch how they put the trash into the truck. Describe what you see.

Offer more complex study-related experiences for **school-age children**.

- Encourage school-age children's interest in the environment and focus on recycling. If you have a garden, start a compost heap and add table scraps.

- Have school-age children learn about recycling in your local community. Where are the recycling sites? What does your community do with the paper and other recyclables that it collects? How much does it collect? Encourage the children to design posters and other marketing materials to encourage their families, neighbors, and schools to recycle.

- Have the children learn about Earth Day and design an Earth Day celebration for your FCC home.

- Investigate how products are packaged in the United States and in other countries. Compare the amount of trash generated. Learn how other communities and countries handle trash, garbage, and recycling.

Summary

This chapter focused on what children are learning and the role you play in building a strong foundation for their success as learners. It showed how the daily routines and the experiences you plan are opportunities for supporting children's learning in language and literacy, math, science, social studies, and the arts. This is not the only chapter where you will find suggestions for promoting children's learning. In chapters 6–20, routines and experiences are discussed in detail. You will find many specific suggestions for selecting materials and for interacting with children as they learn through play. The positive relationships you build with the children in your care are the base from which children acquire cognitive and language skills and knowledge about the world around them. The next chapter, "Caring and Teaching," begins with the important topic of relationships and explains how providers use a range of teaching strategies to guide children's development and learning.

---

[1] From *Heart Start: The Emotional Foundations of School Readiness* (p. 7) by ZERO TO THREE. 1992. Washington, DC: Author. Copyright 1992 by the author. Retrieved April 2009, from http://eric.ed.gov/ERICWebPortal/custom/portlets/recordDetails/detailmini.jsp?_nfpb=true&_&ERICExtSearch_SearchValue_0=ED352171&ERICExtSearch_SearchType_0=no&accno=ED352171. Definitions are reprinted with permission.

[2] Hart, B., & Risley, T. R. (1995). *Meaningful differences in the everyday experiences of young American children*. Baltimore, MD: Brookes Publishing.

[3] Weitzman, E. & Greenberg, J. (2002). *Learning language and loving it* (2nd ed., pp. 37–49). Toronto: The Hanen Centre.

[4] Schickendanz, J. (1999). *Much more than the ABCs: The early stages of reading and writing*. Washington, DC: National Association for the Education of Young Children.

[5] Geist, E. (2004). Infants and toddlers exploring mathematics. In D. Koralek, Ed., *Spotlight on young children and math*. Washington, DC: National Association for the Education of Young Children.

[6] National Council of Teachers of Mathematics. (2000). *Principles and standards for school mathematics*. Reston, VA: Author.

4

Caring and Teaching

Caring and Teaching

Being a family child care provider is interesting, fun, joyful, challenging, educational, inspiring, and often exhausting. No two days are alike. You soothe a crying baby and walk with her snuggled close to your body, letting her know she is safe. You invite some toddlers and twos to sing a song with you, and then you all shout the lyrics together and dance enthusiastically to the music's beat. Outdoors, you hand a preschooler a magnifying glass, show him how to use it to observe the worms under a rock, lead him through the scientific process, and help him test hypotheses. You sit with a school-age child at the computer, helping her locate Web sites that will assist her in doing her homework. During all of these experiences, you use your skills and knowledge to support children's development and learning.

This chapter explores four aspects of your role as a family child care provider:

Building Relationships explains how to build trusting, responsive relationships with and among children while maintaining positive relationships with the members of your own family.

Guiding Children's Behavior suggests ways to help young children express their feelings and regulate their behavior in age-appropriate but acceptable ways. The section describes positive guidance strategies, including creating rules and helping children learn to solve problems. It also provides information about responding to children's challenging behaviors.

Guiding Children's Learning explains how to interact with children and use a variety of teaching strategies to support and extend learning. It also addresses working with children with disabilities and those who are dual-language learners.

Guiding Children's Progress offers guidance about observing children in order to get to know and understand them. This section explains how and why to observe children, what to look for, how to use the information to guide children's progress, and how to share information with families.

Building Relationships

Young children thrive when they have close, supportive, and trusting relationships with the important adults in their lives. Secure relationships are children's foundation for learning. Their connection with you enables them to feel safe enough to move, explore, experiment, and learn. You are in an ideal position for building positive relationships with children because you care for a relatively small number of them in a warm, comfortable environment.

Building Secure Relationships With Children

Every interaction you have with children provides an opportunity to build relationships that enable children to flourish. Here are some strategies for building positive relationships:

Make sure that children's basic needs are met. If you take care of infants, this means feeding them when they're hungry, changing them when their diapers are wet or soiled, and allowing them to rest or sleep when tired. Babies need to be cared for according to their individual timetables, not yours. When infants' needs are met consistently and lovingly, they feel safe enough to explore their environments and get to know new people.

Relate in ways that encourage trust. Be dependable. Let children know that they can count on you. Greet them at the door each morning. Respond promptly to a child who is crying or unhappy. Keep your promises, for example, "Yesterday I said you could help make playdough today. Are you ready?" If you are unable to follow through on a promise for some reason, take time to explain why. Remember that building relationships is a central part of your work. Slow down and spend time with each child individually, every day.

Delight in children's uniqueness and make them feel special. Show that you enjoy every child's company. Laugh with infants as they take their first halting steps, fall, and get up again. Smile at the toddlers' emerging sense of humor. Enjoy the closeness of reading a preschool child's favorite book with her and talking about the story together. Show your pleasure in a school-age child's artistic skills. Express your affection for the children in obvious ways.

Use caring language to let children know that they are respected, understood, and valued. Think about what you say and how you say it. Even infants who cannot yet talk and who do not know the meaning of your words are sensitive to the tone and volume of your voice. Use the children's home languages whenever possible. Practice using caring words and a caring tone. For example, when comforting an upset child, you might say, "You're having a hard time. I can tell by your tears that you're feeling sad. Let's sit together and figure out how to help you feel better."

Be flexible enough to meet individual needs. Offer an infant a bottle when she is hungry, regardless of whether it is the scheduled time for a snack or meal. Give a toddler time to finish his puzzle before you change his diaper. Allow a preschool child to complete the spaceship he is building with LEGO® pieces, even if it means he will not join you as you read a book aloud to a group. Lengthen your outdoor time to accommodate a game the school-age children are playing.

Offer children opportunities to make decisions as often as possible. Give children clear alternatives when a choice is theirs. For example, at snack time, ask younger children to choose banana slices or graham crackers. Allow a school-age child to decide whether to do homework right away or relax for a while before getting started. This shows that you respect children's ability to make decisions on their own.

Observe children closely to decide how to respond. Give the child your full attention. Observe the child's facial expressions and body language. Learn to distinguish an infant's cries so you will know whether the child needs to be fed or needs a different kind of attention from you. Learn how to calm a toddler who is having a tantrum, how to encourage a preschool child to wait for a turn on the tricycle, and how to listen well when a school-age child confides in you about a problem at school.

Build relationships with all children, including those with whom you do not have an easy rapport. You may find that you do not bond with some children as easily as with others. As a professional, you need to understand why. Perhaps you and the child have very different temperaments or personalities. Analyze your feelings and see whether you can change your own attitude or approach to strengthen your relationship with the child. Look for and focus on the child's positive characteristics. Providers often find reward in developing strong relationships with children with whom they do not have a natural rapport. Make a commitment to relate in a positive way with every child in your care, each and every day.

Helping Children Get Along With Other Children

The trusting relationships you build with each child form the foundation for their having other positive relationships. When you treat children in loving, respectful, and consistent ways, children feel good about themselves and their ability to relate well with others. Every child needs to know how to make friends.

Here are some strategies for helping children get along with other children in family child care:

Model friendliness. Young children look to you as a model. They are very aware of what you do, what you say, how you react, and what is important to you. The way you interact with each child, with their families, and with visitors to your program teaches children more powerfully than the words you use. As the old saying goes, "Actions speak louder than words."

Coach children. Show children how to join a group activity. "Nathan, you look like you want to blow bubbles with the other children. I bet they do not know that you want a turn. Try saying, 'May I take a turn?' Go ahead and try it."

Acknowledge children's positive interactions. Comment when you see children engaging positively with each other. Acknowledge when a child uses kind words or otherwise comforts another child. For example, if a toddler comes over to you while you are holding a crying baby, you might say, "You are worried about Jeremy, so you touched his face very gently. You're helping him feel better."

Help children understand the consequences of their actions. Some children do not understand that their actions upset other children. By describing their actions in words, you help children become more conscious of and better able to manage their behavior. For example, you might say, "Keisha, did you notice that you were in the other children's way when you sat down in the middle of the floor? Next time, try asking, 'Where can I play so I'm not in your way?' Let's see if that works better for everyone."

Encourage children to help one another or pair them to work on tasks. Throughout the day, offer children opportunities to assist each other by sharing a job. For example, you might have occasions to invite one child to help look for another's missing shoe, or you might ask two children to set the table for lunch.

Talk with children about making friends. You can spur discussions by reading aloud one of the many wonderful children's books about friendship, such as *Will I Have a Friend?*, by Miriam Cohen, or *The Rainbow Fish*, by Marcus Pfister and T. Allison James.

Point out the benefits of caring behaviors. When you tell a child, "Look at Rosa's smile. She is happy because you invited her to make pretend cupcakes," the child experiences the positive consequences of what he does. Over time, children who practice caring behaviors learn to use them more frequently and without adult prompting.

You may find that some children need more assistance from you than others in making friends. Children who are particularly shy, who are aggressive, or who do not understand other children's emotional cues may need more help from you in building positive relationships. You can help children enter play with others by pointing out how to join the action in a positive way. For example, you might suggest, "When it's time to play outside, let's get your jacket on more quickly so that the other children aren't waiting for you." Model language for children to use when they want to join other children's play, such as saying, "What are you doing? May I help you build a bigger airport?" or "May I help you clean up?" With your guidance, all children can form the positive relationships that are very important to their development and learning in all areas.

Balancing Your Relationships

Providers sometimes worry that their own family will suffer if they get very attached to the FCC children. Indeed, their own children may have moments of jealousy if they see their parent hug and laugh with other children, compliment other children's behavior, and cheer about other children's accomplishments. Even your spouse may experience pangs of jealousy, feeling that you are giving all of your caring and energy to the children in your program.

How do you deal with these feelings, which are quite normal and not unexpected? It often helps to discuss the situation with your family. You need their support and agreement that opening your home and caring for children outside the family is a good decision. It enables you to be at home with your own children and still have a profession. Reassure them that they are your first priority and that the affection you feel for the FCC children is very different from the love you have for them.

Ask your family members to tell you their concerns so that you can address them. Here are a few ideas for helping family members feel more secure.

Invite your family to be part of your FCC program. Family child care is a family affair. Talk about what it means to them to be part of a family child care business. The business will certainly affect their lives. Reassure them that you understand their need for privacy. Help your children see the ways that they benefit from your FCC business, such as having more family income or more children with whom to play. Encourage them to assist as they can, perhaps by helping you put away toys at the end of the day or prepare food for the next day.

Talk to your spouse about his or her role in your family child care program. Will your spouse sometimes be home while children are in your care? If so, does your spouse interact with children easily? How will he or she express affection comfortably? Does your spouse understand positive guidance strategies, and is he or she willing to use them? Would your spouse prefer not to interact with the FCC children but be willing to support you in other ways, such as by grocery shopping, helping with paperwork, repairing broken materials and equipment, cooking dinner, or spending more time with your own children?

Make your family's needs a high priority, especially after family child care hours. You will undoubtedly have program-related things to do after the family child care children leave. These may include thinking about how the day went, reviewing your plans for the next day, tidying up, and preparing meals for the next day. As important as these tasks are, it is essential for you to have time with your family. Do not forget to line up a substitute for the times you may have to take care of important family business or when you or a family member becomes ill.

Maintain your family's rituals and routines. Put your children to bed and wake them up by following your family's established routines. Give your own children special attention every day, whether by reading a book together, watching a video, or going outside at night to look at the stars.

Help your own children understand how they belong to the family child care program. If your own children are part of the program, help them manage sharing their home, their toys, and their parent's attention with others. For example, if most toys are to be shared, consider letting them choose some that will not be shared. Help them understand that, even though they are your own special children, they must follow the FCC rules during FCC hours.

Take care of yourself. Despite the hard work, being a family child care provider should be an enjoyable experience. Find ways to relax and reduce your stress when you are having a difficult day or things do not go as well as planned. Take a deep breath. Do yoga with the children. Although you strive to be an excellent and professional family child care provider, it is realistic to expect missteps from which you can learn.

Guiding Children's Behavior

Children learn what is expected of them by observing the behavior of the people around them. Children sometimes behave inappropriately when they do not understand or cannot meet adult expectations. Some children act out when forced to follow a schedule that conflicts with their natural rhythms. Others are confused when rules and routines are different from those at home. With adult guidance, children learn to identify their emotions, use language to express strong feelings, and think about consequences before acting.

The words *punishment* and *discipline* are sometimes mistakenly used to mean the same thing. They are actually very different. Punishment is a response to unwanted behavior that places a penalty on the child. Punishment may stop children's negative behavior temporarily, but it does not teach them to manage their behavior, themselves. Discipline means directing children toward acceptable behavior so they learn to control their own actions. Because discipline is often confused with punishment, the early childhood field often uses the word *guidance* instead of *discipline*. Guidance requires an understanding of child development.

Age-Appropriate Expectations

Knowing what is reasonable to expect of young children at each stage of development helps you know how to respond to children and how to help them understand their feelings and manage their behavior. Some child behaviors that bother family child care providers are actually signs of typical development.

Infants are just beginning to understand that their actions affect other people. As they explore the world, some of their explorations have results that adults do not want. For example, a 5-month old child who rolls from back to tummy may cry because he cannot turn back over again. Infants do not yet have the ability to think consciously about what they are doing or how to express their feelings in acceptable ways. Until they are at least 6–8 months old, infants cannot control their own behavior. They cry to let you know they are hungry, tired, or uncomfortable. They are not crying to annoy or control you deliberately. Comfort them by meeting their needs consistently and lovingly. That helps them learn how to calm themselves and regulate their emotions.

Mobile infants begin to realize that adults do not approve of some of the things they do. They begin to use your facial expressions, body language, and "I statements" to guide their behavior. A simple smile gives the message, "Yes, it's all right to splash in the tray of water that is on the floor." Even from across the room a frown can stop a child from throwing a block.

Toddlers are full of energy and eager to assert their independence. They are just beginning to use language to express their feelings. They want to do things independently even if they are not skilled enough. They often test limits and enjoy the power of saying, "No!" even to something they want. They can be possessive and are not yet ready to share. They need adults who understand them; have a sense of humor; and who set clear, realistic limits about which behaviors are acceptable and which are not. Positive reminders help toddlers behave appropriately.

Preschool children are beginning to understand the difference between right and wrong. They can use speech to express their feelings and to solve problems, although they do not always do so. They sometimes act out their feelings or lose control without considering the consequences of their actions. Preschool children need understanding adults to help them use speech, not their hands or feet, to express anger and frustration.

School-age children know the differences between appropriate and inappropriate behavior. However, they are still children, and they sometimes act irresponsibly. At about age 8, they gain an understanding of right and wrong. They are interested in rules and are very concerned about whether problems are handled fairly. They are usually able to tell an adult what is bothering them, and they often offer solutions.

Supporting the Development of Self-Regulation

An important part of growing up is learning how to behave in the ways expected by one's family and community. Children need a lot of time and experience to develop self-regulation, which is the ability to manage feelings and control actions. Young children have intense feelings of joy and excitement as well as feelings of anger and frustration. They do not always have the ability to stop and think about how to express their feelings in appropriate ways.

You can do many things to help children develop and practice self-regulation skills.

Give children opportunities to plan and to follow guidelines. Planning helps children decide what they will do and when. Playing games with rules, using recipe cards to cook, and making wooden bead necklaces with color patterns also support children's self-regulation skills.

Encourage children's sense of independence. Invite children to demonstrate their skills. For example, you might say, "The drawing DVD is on the computer table. Feel free to load the program and use it any time you'd like."

Offer acceptable choices. Choices give children some control over events. Offer them many opportunities to make choices about what to play with, wear, and eat so that they know that they have the power to make choices and that their choices are important to you. Make sure that the offered choices are acceptable to you and reasonable for the child. For example, you might ask, "Would you rather play with the cardboard blocks or paint at the easel while we wait for the other children to finish their naps?" Limit choices for very young children to two alternatives.

Give children plenty of opportunities to develop competence. Invite children to help you with everyday chores, such as setting the table, preparing food, and sorting laundry. Label shelves so children can find what they want and help put materials away. Interpret children's cues to understand what they want to communicate, and respond to children's attempts to express themselves.

Read aloud books that are related to self-regulation. Choose time-honored books that children love, such as *Please, Baby, Please,* by Spike Lee and Tonya Lewis Lee; *When Sophie Gets Angry, Really, Really Angry,* by Molly Bang; *I Ain't Gonna Paint No More,* by Karen Beaumont; *Lily's Purple Plastic Purse,* by Kevin Henke; *Quentin Fenton Herter III,* by Amy MacDonald; *The Grouchy Ladybug,* by Eric Carle; and *It's Hard to be Five: Learning How to Work My Control Panel,* by Jamie Lee Curtis and Laura Cornell.

Play games that encourage self-regulation. Is it any wonder that so many children's games provide opportunities for children to practice stopping or controlling an action? Play "Statues" and encourage children to stop moving completely when the music stops. "Simon Says" requires children to think before they act. In the game "Mother, May I?" children must ask for and receive permission before they move.

Using Positive Guidance Strategies

Positive guidance means encouraging appropriate behavior and minimizing unwanted behavior. You can act in two ways: 1) to prevent or minimize problem behaviors, and 2) to teach children which behaviors are appropriate and which are not. Both kinds of adult action help young children learn to manage their feelings and monitor their own behavior.

Children's behaviors are affected by the way the environment is structured, the amount and types of materials, and the daily schedule and routines. These factors are discussed in chapter 2, "Organizing Your Home and Your Day." You can minimize unwanted behaviors by adjusting daily routines to minimize noise, confusion, and waiting times. Here are some ways to set up your environment and schedule to help prevent unwanted behavior:

Set up an interesting, safe space that children may explore freely without your constantly having to say, "No." Make the environment as free of frustration as possible. Offer toys, games, and puzzles that gently challenge the changing abilities of the children in your care. Always make available some familiar materials that the children have played with successfully.

Establish and maintain a consistent daily schedule. Having a predictable day allows children to know what to expect next and provides the sense of order upon which they depend.

Build cleanup time into the daily schedule. Being able to participate in cleanup without being prompted is a sign of self-regulation.

Allow enough time for children to run and play outdoors. Look at your daily schedule to make sure that children have outdoor play time in the morning and afternoon. If necessary, adjust your schedule to allow more time.

Provide unstructured time for pretend play every day. Researchers have found that one of the best ways for children to develop self-regulation skills is through daily dramatic play. Encourage children to use imaginary props and allow them to play for at least an hour a day.

Anticipate children's physical needs. Serve lunch before children get too hungry. Help children take naps before they become overly tired. Give them a chance to play outdoors when they are ready for active play.

You can also minimize problematic behaviors and encourage acceptable behaviors by the ways you interact with children. Think about the situation from the children's perspective before intervening. For example, be aware that what looks like one child's grabbing a toy from another child may be a game of "taking away and giving back." Here are some additional guidelines:

Remember that children may not be able to use speech to communicate their needs. Learn to read their nonverbal cues, such as gestures. As they grow older, help them use speech by telling them what they might say and encouraging them to practice saying it.

Use simple, clear language to communicate acceptable behaviors. For example, explain, "You may use the crayons on the paper, but not on the wall." Let your facial expression and tone of voice emphasize your message.

Acknowledge children's positive behavior by describing their actions when they show self-control. For example, say, "You let Jorge finish the puzzle before you tried doing it."

Be specific. Avoid giving empty praise. Instead of telling a child, "Good job," encourage him by explaining exactly what he did and why it is appropriate. For example, explain, "You put your dirty dishes in the sink. Now I'll be able to wash them quickly. When everyone helps clean up, it makes lunchtime more pleasant for all of us."

Tell children what they may do, rather than what they may not do. For example, say, "If you want to listen to music, please put on the headphones. The children near you are trying to look at books, so they need the room to be quiet."

Acknowledge children's feelings and help children express them appropriately. For example, explain, "I know that you are angry. That's okay, but people must not hit each other. When you feel angry, say 'I'm mad.' Then I will help you."

Share your feelings about particular behaviors. For example, explain, "When you hit other children, I feel worried."

Use the word *no* sparingly. Save this for dangerous situations so it will be effective.

Model appropriate behavior by being kind and respectful at all times. For example, ask, "Will you please help me carry these extra scarves outside? That way, if anyone gets cold, no one will have to go back indoors to get one. Thank you very much."

Learn what comforts each child. Be sensitive to cultural differences. Offer hugs and cuddles to children who are comfortable with them. If you or particular children are uncomfortable with cuddling, find other ways to express your caring. You might comfort a child by getting down on his or her level, by making eye contact, by singing, or by simply sitting near a child without actually touching. Some children look forward to a "high five" or bumping fists. Be aware that families express affection in different ways, and that, just because a particular way is different, it can be as warm and nurturing as another way.

Use your sense of humor. You can use humor to deflect tension, energize a child, and win his cooperation. For example, you might ask, "Will you please help me pick up these puzzle pieces? A tornado must have come through here while we were in the bathroom."

When you take a positive approach to guiding children's behavior, you help children learn self-control, solve problems on their own, and treat others with kindness and respect.

Developing Rules

Rules and limits help both teachers and children agree on what behavior is acceptable. You can involve children in setting general rules. When children help set the limits, they are more likely to understand, remember, and follow them.

Develop a few positively worded rules for your family child care program. Think about what rules are important to you. It may be helpful to think about categories of rules first, instead of the actual rules. These might include rules for reaching these goals:

- maintaining physical safety
- respecting the rights of others
- not hurting others' feelings
- caring for the family child care home and materials

Using the categories as guidelines, you might then develop four simple rules like these:

- Be safe.
- Help each other.
- Be kind to others.
- Keep our home neat.

The "big rule–little rule" strategy can help children remember and apply the general rules in a particular situation. To guide a child's behavior, state one of your four main rules (the big rule) and pair it with a very specific behavior that you want to encourage (the little rule). Here are some examples:

- Be safe. Keep your bottom in the chair when you are sitting.
- Be kind to others. Sit on the floor so everyone can see the book.

To begin the process of setting rules, talk with children about the consequences of their behavior. For example, ask, "What might happen if someone squirts water on the floor?" Children can point out that someone might fall. Responding to this, you might tell them that there is a need for a rule to "Keep water where it belongs. Keep it in the sink, in a tray, or in a tub."

Post the rules where you and the children can see them. Remind children about the rules and review them regularly. As children develop, they can handle more choices, more activities, and more responsibilities. In response, you will need to review and revise the rules in your home. It is also all right to individualize rules and limits to meet a child's needs. "If you do not want to join us in reading a book, you may do puzzles or draw a picture."

Teaching Children to Solve Problems

Conflicts and disagreements are a normal part of life in family child care, so it is helpful to encourage preschool and school-age children to solve problems on their own. Children will need social problem-solving skills throughout their lives. By teaching children problem-solving skills, you let them know that you think that they are able to solve problems and that you expect them to take responsibility for doing so. It also helps keep conflicts from getting worse.

There are four steps in the problem-solving process:

1. **Identify the problem.** For example, perhaps children who are building with blocks are interfering with children who are playing a board game on the floor.

2. **Brainstorm possible solutions.** Invite children to share ideas about how to solve the problem. Invite everyone involved to contribute a suggestion. You can write down all the ideas on chart paper and then go over them with the children. In the example, perhaps the children will suggest moving the board game to a table, closing the block area when children are playing board games, or telling the children who are playing the board game to play it at a different time.

3. **Agree on a solution.** Restate the children's ideas and ask them to think about the best way to solve the problem. Clarify what the children will do to test the possible solution. Make sure everyone has the same understanding. "Here's what I think you decided: We'll move the board game to the dining room table so Rosa and Nathan can play it while Keisha and Jorge are building with blocks. See if you agree."

4. **Try the solution and see how well it works.** Remember to give the solution enough time to work. If the original solution doesn't solve the problem, help the children test another possibility. (Fortunately, the solution in the example worked!)

This process can be used when two children disagree and for resolving problems that involve more children. Model the process when you resolve problems with children and help children use this process as often as possible when conflicts arise.

Stopping Unwanted Behavior

While positive guidance sets a tone for managing children's behavior, it does not always prevent challenging behavior. This is especially true if you have toddlers or young preschoolers in your program who have a developmental need to test limits—and your patience! They want to be independent, but they still haven't mastered the skills they need to do things on their own. This is a normal part of development, and your role is to support their skill development.

These are the most common types of unwanted behavior:

Testing limits is one of the ways children discover how much power they have and the kind of authority with which they are dealing. Some children test limits repeatedly, and they need adults to understand why children test limits.

Physical aggression includes such behavior as hitting, scratching, and kicking. Physical aggression must be stopped immediately.

Temper tantrums are a child's way of expressing frustration by screaming, kicking, and crying. Tantrums often occur when children have very strong feelings that they cannot express through words or when they are frustrated because they cannot control a situation. Tantrums are not fun for anyone. They can leave children feeling exhausted and frightened at their loss of control. They can also make adults feel angry, incompetent, and even embarrassed.

Biting is common in groups of young children. It is always upsetting and can be frightening for children, parents, and providers alike. Like other forms of physical aggression, it must be stopped immediately.

Bullying is a way some children exert control over others. Bullies are often the most insecure children. Bullies sometimes pick on particular children. They know which children will not stand up for themselves, so they disrupt the more timid children's play, grab their toys, and push them around. Bullying must be stopped and redirected. The longer children get their way by bullying others, the harder it is to change that behavior. Children who are victimized time after time can become targets of other types of aggression and suffer from low self-esteem.

Respond immediately to unwanted behavior. Remember that both the aggressor and the victim need your positive attention. When adults pay too much attention to the victim, the aggressive child feels isolated and guilty and may continue to be aggressive in order get attention.

- Comfort the child who was hurt. When appropriate, give first aid (e.g., apply a Band-Aid® or treat a bite).
- State clearly that hitting, kicking, or biting is not all right and that it breaks your program rule of being kind to one another. Speak firmly and seriously. Avoid being overly dramatic so that your response doesn't make the aggressive act more interesting and appealing.
- Help children regain control.
- Involve the aggressive child in comforting the child who was hurt (if the injured child permits this). This gives the aggressive child an opportunity to help and to stop being an aggressor. Use these moments to teach caring behavior. Remember that it is scary for a child to be so out of control that he or she hurts someone. Teach victims of bullying to be assertive when an incident occurs.

- If a child is having a tantrum, keep the child from hurting himself or someone else. Assure the child that you will help him. After he has calmed down, acknowledge his feelings in ways that show you accept him and his feelings: "Not being able to finish that puzzle really frustrated you! It is scary to be so angry."

- Document serious incidents, especially bites.

- Acknowledge your own feelings so you do not add more tension to the situation. Of course you are upset when a child is hurt, but children are quick to notice your feelings. Biting may be particularly frustrating for you because it can occur despite your preventive measures.

When children lose control, you can help them compose themselves by modeling calm behavior. Keep in mind that you cannot help children develop self-control if you are out of control, yourself. Screaming at children, isolating them with a time-out system, taking away privileges, and making them feel incompetent rarely produce positive results and often increase and prolong unwanted behaviors. **Physical punishment is never, ever acceptable**. Use positive guidance strategies to avoid power struggles.

Talk about unwanted behaviors at neutral times. Help children practice strategies for stopping their own unwanted behavior and reacting to the unwanted behavior of other children. While "time out" is a punitive rather than positive guidance strategy, you can redirect a child by helping her take a deep breath, move away from the situation, and find something calming to do, such as playing at the water table. Remember that no single approach works for every child or every situation and that it takes time for children to learn how to regulate their own behavior. The positive guidance strategies you use will help most children learn these skills over time.

Addressing Ongoing Behavioral Problems

What should you do if a child in your family child care program behaves in challenging ways repeatedly and does not seem to respond to your positive guidance strategies? The unwanted behaviors prevent the child from fully participating in and benefitting from the program. The behaviors are challenging both to the other children in the program and to you. You will have to figure out when they occur and what might be causing them. With that information, you and the child's family can develop a plan of action.

Keep in mind that a reason underlies all challenging behaviors. Challenging behaviors are often cries for help. Children who behave in challenging ways again and again may not know how to express their feelings in other ways.

To deal with challenging behaviors, make and carry out an ongoing prevention and intervention plan. Here are some steps you can take:

1. **Observe carefully to identify when the behavior occurs.** Every time there is an incident, write down the time of day that the behavior occurred, who was involved, and what preceded the unwanted behavior. Use objective, descriptive terms that do not label or judge the child. For example, write, "S was washing a doll in the water table. L went over to S and bit S on the arm. S screamed. L took the doll S was holding and began to play with it." Be sure to date your note.

2. **Talk with the child's family.** The child's family may know about events at home or in the neighborhood that may be upsetting their child. With the family's input and permission, it is sometimes appropriate to seek help from an outside expert. Talking with families and specialists about challenging behaviors enables you to collaborate with them in providing the best care for the child at your program and at home.

3. **Review and analyze the information to determine patterns and the causes of the behavior.** Systematic observations over time reveal a great deal of valuable information about when and why the child engages in the behavior. Note such things as the time of day; what else is going on at the time; and other factors, such as whether the child came late or is not feeling well. This information can often help you prevent unwanted behavior. For instance, if you notice that Nathan often hits Keisha when he is frustrated because she cannot understand his speech, you can restate what he is trying to say to Keisha. If Jorge has tantrums at around 11:00 in the morning, you can think about whether he is hungry, tired at that time, or needs some time away from the group. Depending upon what you think is causing his recurring tantrums, you can give him an early lunch or an early nap, or spend some one-on-one time with him.

4. **Develop and implement a plan.** Together, you and the family can develop a consistent plan for responding to the behavior and teaching the child better ways to express strong feelings. It is very important to tell the child that he or she is still cared about and loved, even if the behavior is unacceptable. Most children want to learn how to behave in acceptable ways because they want you to like them and they do not want to disappoint their families.

5. **Assess progress.** Maintain regular contact with the family so that you can evaluate how well your plan is working and make any necessary adjustments. Change takes time, and it takes some children longer than others. If a challenging behavior continues for a long time, you might—with the family's input and permission—want to consult with an outside expert. You do not have to handle particularly challenging behaviors on your own.

Guiding children's behavior may sometimes appear to be occupying a great deal of your time. Remember that, as you help children learn to regulate their behavior, you build a solid foundation for their positive interactions with others and for their academic learning.

Guiding Children's Learning

Everything you do with children during the day is an opportunity to guide their learning. Think about the routines you follow each day. As you change a baby's diaper and talk to him about what you are doing and how the day is going, he learns language and learns to trust you. When you ask all of the children with laces on their shoes to put their coats on for a neighborhood walk, you are teaching children classification skills and giving them practice in following directions. When you ask children to help you set the table for lunch, they learn to understand one-to-one correspondence and spatial relationships.

Particular types of activities offer particular opportunities for you to teach content. When children observe a caterpillar and you talk with them about how it moves and what it eats, they gain scientific knowledge. When they arrange community worker figurines throughout a block city they built and you talk about the jobs people do, they learn about social studies. When they look at books and retell the stories, they learn language and literacy skills. As they measure ingredients for bread dough, children learn math and motor skills. As they bake the dough and talk with you about how materials change states, they learn more science.

Helping children learn and apply new concepts, develop important skills, and gain knowledge about the world is one of your major responsibilities as a family child care provider. You help children become enthusiastic and active learners when you use these strategies:

Set up the environment so that it promotes safe exploration.

Encourage children to make predictions, experiment, and draw conclusions.

Encourage children to try new things.

Expect children to make mistakes and learn from them.

Allow children time to learn and practice new skills.

Build on children's interests.

Take children's individual temperaments and learning styles into account.

Listen to what children have to say and respond appropriately.

Ask children questions that stretch their thinking.

Learning Through Play

Young children learn through play. As they engage in pretend play, create block structures, work with puzzles and other toys, listen to music, look at books and retell stories, play outside, experiment with natural materials like sand and water, prepare snacks, and work on the computer, they learn about the world, explore concepts, and gain knowledge and skills. When children take the initiative as they play, they choose where to play, share ideas about roles and scenarios, and try them. However, this does not mean that providers do nothing but watch. You have an important role in facilitating children's play.

You set the stage for children's learning by selecting materials that engage children and stretch their thinking. You provide guidance when children need help, ask questions to support children's thinking, and encourage them to approach learning actively. In a choice-time period, a child might choose to work on a puzzle, build a block tower, look through a familiar book and retell the story, or play a game with a friend. When children are free to follow their interests in an environment that supports and extends their exploration, they progress in all developmental areas.

Children play throughout the day during routines and experiences. Here are some examples of what children are learning:

- Jeremy (8 months) pulls himself up and leans against the coffee table so that he is standing. He reaches for the snow globe that is on table. He picks it up, shakes the globe, and laughs as he watches the snow. He is developing motor skills and learning about cause and effect.

- Tamika (19 months) and Jorge (2 ½ years) are sitting with you on the couch as you read *Click, Clack, Moo: Cows That Type* together. Jorge complains that he cannot see the pictures. You move Tamika over slightly and reposition the book, and Tamika accepts the new arrangement. She is cooperating in a group situation.

- Jorge (2 ½ years) punches a hole in a ball of playdough and pretends to eat it. You ask him, "Did you enjoy that, Jorge?" "Si", he responds, "I like donas". He is learning to express his thoughts in two languages.

- Nathan (3 years) strings colorful wooden beads on a knotted string. He holds the beaded string around his neck and says "Exess." "Necklace," you confirm enthusiastically. "You made a necklace with red, blue, and green beads." Nathan is refining fine motor skills and learning to speak.

- Rosa (4 years) is dressed up as a doctor and pretending to give Nathan a shot. She tells him. "It's okay. No te duele". She is learning to work through her fears by taking on the role of a doctor and controlling the situation. She is beginning to form sentences in English and continuing to use her Spanish skills.

- Keisha (4 ½ years) is at the kitchen table, using a recipe card to make nachos as you supervise. Keisha is learning to be independent, master self-help skills, follow directions, and begin to read.

- Tyrone (8 years) is sitting at a picnic table outside, looking through the book *Birds of North America* and writing down the names of birds he has seen in the neighborhood. He is studying the characteristics of living things, reading, and writing.

Guiding Children's Play

Your intentional interactions with children promote meaningful learning through play. While it is important to set up the environment, provide interesting materials, and have an appropriate schedule, your interactions with children support their learning in even more important ways. The questions you ask and the other strategies you use to extend learning are critical. Like all early childhood teachers, FCC providers teach with intention. They are purposeful. They understand **what** and **how** to teach. They make learning **meaningful** to children, and they use **specific strategies** to guide children's learning.

FCC providers make learning purposeful by knowing what children should be learning. Chapter 3, "What Children Are Learning," explains what children of different ages learn in the areas of literacy, math, science, social studies, and the arts. Providers make learning meaningful to children by helping them build on what they already know, by promoting children's problem-solving skills, by offering tools and materials, and by encouraging children to interact with others.

Providers use these five teaching strategies to guide children's learning:

1. **Acknowledge and describe.** To validate what children are doing and to make them more aware of their thought processes and actions, tell them what you notice:

   - "You are playing with an interesting group of animals. We would expect to see all of them on a farm, except for one animal. Which animal would you not expect to find on a farm?"

   - "I see that you are mixing yellow and blue paint. I wonder what new color you will create."

   - "When you clicked the computer mouse, the dog in the picture started to run."

2. **Coach.** To sustain their attention, encourage children and offer suggestions.

   - "That puzzle piece just doesn't seem to fit. I wonder what would happen if you turned it. Can you find another piece that has the same color? Do you think it's the boy's arm? Where would an arm go?"

   - "Cutting with scissors is hard. Let's see if I can help you by putting my hand on top of yours. We can try cutting together."

3. **Extend.** To extend children's thinking, offer additional materials, ask open-ended questions, and give other open-ended prompts. The best questions encourage children to give more than a one- or two-word answer. They are open-ended, which means that many answers are correct. They encourage children to consider consequences, make predictions, and apply what they already know to new situations. Open-ended questions challenge children's thinking and lead to more meaningful learning.

   - "What can we bring outside to use as bubble frames?"

   - "There aren't any more blocks on the shelf. That's for sure. What else can you use to finish your building?"

   - "Why is he wearing boots when it's not raining?"

   - "What can you do to keep the paint from dripping on the floor?"

   - "Where do you think those clouds are going?"

   - "What would happen if there were no cars, trucks, buses, planes or boats? How would we get around?"

4. **Demonstrate.** Model a skill or behavior for children to imitate.

  • "When we cut with a knife, we put the sharp side of the blade down. We hold the knife by the handle. We make sure that our other fingers are out of the way. Watch me first. Then you may try it."

5. **Give information.** Provide facts, model language, and help children find answers to their questions. For example, when you are reading *Caps for Sale,* explain, "A peddler is a person who sells things. The things the peddler sells are called *wares.*"

These teaching strategies are used throughout the day as you guide learning during daily routines and experiences, during transitions, and when you gather a small group of children for a planned activity.

Including All Children

All children can thrive in your program. Some providers think they have to do something dramatically different to accommodate children with disabilities or children who are dual-language learners. This is not usually the case. As you develop relationships with children and use a variety of instructional strategies, you will be able to judge how children respond and which strategies work best in which situations.

Teaching Children With Disabilities

Children with disabilities need to be included and successful. Your general knowledge about child development and your specific knowledge about the children in your care can be applied to your work with children who have diagnosed disabilities or other special needs. As you support each child's development and learning, you must look beyond the specific diagnosis to see how the disability affects the particular child. You must not generalize about a child on the basis of his or diagnosis. Here are some guidelines:

See the child as a child first. Learn about each child's strengths and interests first, and then consider the child's special needs. Use language that shows your understanding of this. For example, speak about a child with autism, rather than an autistic child. The difference is significant. It reflects your philosophy about children with disabilities.

Learn about the effects of a specific disability to decide what, if any, adjustments you need to make. Here are some examples.

  • A child with a visual impairment relies more heavily on her senses of hearing and touch for communication. When offered choices, it will be helpful for her to touch each item and hear about the choices.

  • A child with a hearing impairment relies heavily on his sense of sight for communication. It may be useful for you to learn sign language and to use cards with pictures of routines, experiences, and materials so that you can communicate with him.

- A child with a brain injury may need more time to think about what you are saying and more time to transition from one activity to another. Slowing your conversations and actions may help engage this child.

- A child with physical limitations needs you to free the environment of barriers that would restrict his or her mobility. When you help her move, she will feel respected if you explain what you are doing and why.

Work closely with the child's family. The parents of a child with a disability are your greatest sources of support and information. Ask them to share what they know about their child's interests and how the child's disability affects what he or she can do. Invite them to share tips and strategies they use at home, especially those that have been taught to them by a special educator.

Work with a specialist. Depending on the child's age, a child with a diagnosed disability will have either an Individualized Family Service Plan (for children birth to age 3) or an Individualized Education Program (ages 3–21). (See chapter 1.) Many objectives on these plans will be the similar to those you have for all children, so many of the strategies you use as you care for the child with disabilities will fit easily into your regular plans and daily schedule. For other objectives, you might need to add special toys and adaptive equipment, or you might need to change strategies (such as blinking the lights to catch the attention of a deaf child). These adaptations and strategies should be included in the child's plan. As with all children, observe continually with the objectives for development and learning in mind and adapt equipment, materials, and teaching strategies as necessary.

With parental permission, work with the child's specialist(s) to develop strategies that will work in your program. Be sure to share information with the specialist about the daily routines and experiences in your program and talk to the specialist about ways that all children can participate in activities suggested for the child with disabilities. Encourage the specialist to find opportunities to support the child's development and learning in the family child care environment.

Encourage, but do not force, appropriate independence. Some children need extra support to develop skills and self-confidence. Help children with disabilities play with other children. Remember that sometimes children with disabilities do not initiate play as often as other children. They may need more support and opportunities to practice entering social play.

Use peer buddies as teaching models. This technique not only facilitates interaction, but it also builds the peer-mentoring capabilities of children who have strengths in particular developmental areas.

Supporting Dual-Language Learners

Some children in your program may be learning more than one language at the same time or learning another language sequentially. In our example, Jorge (2 ½ years) is learning both English and Spanish at the same time. Rosa (4 years) already speaks

Spanish and is learning to speak English now that she is at FCC. You can support children who are dual-language learners by using these strategies:

Learn some words in the children's home languages and, if possible, label materials and storage places in those languages as well as in English. Seeing and hearing their home languages will help children feel welcome and safe in an environment where people speak a different language.

Use concrete objects and gestures to communicate with children while they are nonverbal. Keep in mind that they are actively learning, observing, and making sense of what is going on around them. Help them feel included in your program.

Use objects and hands-on experiences to help children understand language and make the transition from nonverbal communication to using a few words. Focus on the child's intent, and extend or repeat what the child says.

Encourage children who are dual-language learners and children whose home language is English to play together. Children can engage in dramatic play, catch and throw balls with each other, move to music, and dig and bury objects in sand even if they speak different languages.

Encourage nonverbal communication. Remember that children understand more than they are able to say. Let children show you how much they understand by following directions that call for an action (for example, standing up, sitting down, turning around, running, walking, or jumping). Ask questions to which children can respond by pointing to, picking up, showing, or giving something. Use pictures, props, and other visual cues to help children understand.

Offer encouragement and, as children feel more confident, support conversations in English. Avoid correcting the child's grammar but model correct language as you speak and read aloud. Do not be concerned if the child mixes languages, even in the same sentence.

Build your relationship with each child. Play with children. Have fun together. Be patient. Give children time to express themselves, and be careful not to rush them.

Provide books in the children's home languages if possible. If you do not understand the language, scan illustrations and lengths of the texts to see if they look appropriate.

Incorporate pictures and familiar objects that will help the children feel comfortable in your FCC home. For example, if appropriate for the children in your group, add a tortilla press for dramatic play and use one in the kitchen. Offer familiar music and dances. Include dress-up clothes from children's home cultures as appropriate.

Involve families by encouraging them to continue speaking their primary languages when they visit your program. Invite them to record books on tape or to help make signs and books for the program in their home languages.

Keep in mind that your attitude is very important. If you value and support multilingualism, all children will benefit, not only those whose home languages are other than English.

Guiding Children's Progress

Tamika (19 months) is a curious toddler with boundless energy and a zest for exploring the world. She is beginning to express her curiosity verbally, asking simple questions, such as "Ball?" She expresses her needs with simple sentences like "Up, p'ease," and she lets you know just how she feels about something by declaring, "No!" She likes to pretend to call her mother on the play phone. She smiles every day when her friend Nathan arrives at the program, and she squeals with delight every afternoon when her brother Tyrone arrives from school.

You watched her as she learned to turn over, sit, pull up to standing, take her first steps, babble, and say her first words. You were fascinated as you watched her develop and learn. You noticed each new thing she did, thought about what she was likely to do next, and planned activities to guide her progress. This process of observing children and finding out what they know and can do is called *assessment*. An assessment system provides a way to be intentional about how you guide children's learning and share information with families. The first step in guiding children's progress is to collect facts. We collect facts by observing children, organizing a portfolio, and talking to children's families.

Observing Children

Best practices in early childhood education require providers to observe each child across all areas of development and to use their observations to inform their practice. The information they collect helps them decide how to set up the physical environment and structure the day, how to plan for individual children on the basis of each child's interests and skills, and how to interact spontaneously with children throughout the day. The objectives for development and learning guide your observations by helping you think about what to look for. (See the "Introduction," chapters 1 and 3, and the "Appendix.") You use the information from your observations in your ongoing planning, as described in chapter 2. You also share information with families to help each other build a more complete understanding of how their children are developing and learning. (See chapter 5.)

Children develop and learn best in programs that respond to their individual skills and interests. Observing children is one of the best ways to get the information you need. Observation tells you about children's skills and interests as well as how they handle frustrations, get involved in group play, and cope with separation. Children change over time, so observation is an ongoing process.

Observation is the act of watching and listening to a child. You observe children every day. For example, you notice Jeremy using his thumb and forefinger to eat breakfast cereal. You see that Nathan's blowing on his warm cereal has helped him learn to make the sound of the letter *f* and that Tyrone likes to spend a few minutes with his sister, Tamika, when he arrives in the afternoon.

You observe children for a variety of reasons:

- to determine each child's interests, strengths, and needs: "Nathan uses the tongs nearly every day to sort buttons."
- to meet individual needs: "Tyrone has completed every jigsaw puzzle we have. I need to offer him more challenging puzzles."
- to document progress: "The recording I made of Rosa's conversation documents how many English words she learned in the last month."
- to determine the cause of a challenging behavior: "According to my notes, it appears that Tamika has started hitting other children when they are playing with something she wants."
- to report children's progress to families: "As you know, I've been encouraging Jorge to sleep during nap time. My notes from the last two weeks indicate that there was only one day when he didn't go right to sleep."

A careful, organized approach to observation helps you collect accurate and useful information. You observe constantly and write brief notes whenever you can. Observe children as you work with them throughout the day, paying attention to what they do and say. For instance, you might make a batch of playdough with a group of children. As you follow a picture recipe, you can note which children are able to count the number of cups and tablespoons, and you can pay attention to the kinds of questions children ask and answer.

If you keep some file cards or sticky notes handy, you can record what you see and hear immediately. Later, you will organize your notes, look at your notes with the objectives for development and learning in mind, and summarize the information so you can use it to plan and to communicate with families.

Recording observations in an objective and accurate way takes practice. Useful written observation notes contain just the facts. Begin with the date, time, and setting. Record what the child does and says. Note only what you can see and hear, not what you think the child wants to do, why he is doing something, or the idea that he will not do something.

Factual observation notes might

- describe actions: "Jeremy crawled to the toy shelf, sat up, reached for a clutch ball, took it off the shelf, and squeezed it."
- include quotations: "Keisha said, 'My grandma works in the Empire State Building.'"
- describe gestures: "Jorge pointed to the bird that landed on the windowsill."
- describe facial expressions: "Tamika smiled when Tyrone came over and said hello to her."
- describe creations: "Rosa rolled out the playdough to form a big circle. She put small spheres all over the top of the circle."

Objective observation notes do not include interpretations, impressions, assumptions, or judgments. When your notes include words like *shy, aggressive, upset, hyperactive,* or *angry,* they reveal your impressions, interpretations, or assumptions rather than what a child actually did or said. These judgmental words may or may not tell an accurate story. Interpretations, impressions, or assumptions include

- labels (*shy, vivacious, creative*)
- intentions (*wants to*)
- evaluations (*good job*)
- judgments (*beautiful, sloppy*)
- negatives (*did not, cannot, will not*)

Writing objective notes takes practice. The more aware you are of what objective notes include, the more skilled you will become at writing them.

Make writing observation notes as easy as possible. Carry some sticky notes and a pen or pencil so you can write things down as you notice them. You do not have to write a long paragraph. Write quick notes, using short phrases and abbreviations. Be sure to note the date, time, and setting. Briefly describe what the child did and said, capturing the child's words if possible.

An example of an observation note about Tamika is presented on the left.

Analyzing and interpreting your observation notes comes later, when you plan for individual children and your group.

3/18 – Circle time. T on my lap, singing "Thumbkin." T put up hands one at a time when I sang, "Here I am." Put hands behind back one at a time for "Run away." Said, "Run 'way." Walked away from circle after song. Came back. Said, "sing."

Keeping Portfolios

Another way to gather information about children is by organizing portfolios. A portfolio is a purposeful collection of items that shows a child's efforts in various developmental areas. The items are examples of a child's efforts, achievements, and learning style, and they show a child's development and learning. To show a child's progress, it is important to collect similar samples over time. For example, photos that show a child eating finger foods, holding a spoon, and later scooping vegetables from a serving bowl are an excellent way to document the child's fine-motor skill development.

Think of two or three types of items that would document learning in each developmental area. If you're comfortable with and have access to the necessary equipment, you can photocopy or scan children's scribbles and writing; take photographs to capture a child's involvement in an activity; audiotape a child's use of language; or videotape a child engaged in pretend play, reading a book, or giving a doll a bath. Be sure to date the portfolio items and write a brief description of each. Think of convenient ways to store portfolios. Providers use everything from empty pizza boxes to accordion files, magazine files, and hanging file folders. Choose whatever system will be most efficient for you.

Here are some ideas about what to include a child's portfolio:

- drawings, paintings, collages, and other artwork
- writing (marks on paper, scribbles, labels, letters, names and other words, numerals, signs and other messages)
- a story dictated to you and illustrated by the child, or a book made entirely by the child
- printouts of the child's computer work
- graphs and drawings related to a science experiment
- recordings of a baby's babbling, cooing, and saying first words; recordings of the child singing; or recordings of an older child's dramatic play dialogue and storytelling
- photos of the child's block buildings

You can use portfolios for several purposes:

- to share information with families: "It's easy to see Rosa's progress when we compare the drawings she made 6 months ago with the drawings she is making now."

- to review a child's progress, set new goals, and plan experiences: "This video shows Keisha telling an imaginative story with several plots. I want to work with her to help her expand her skills so her stories are easier to understand."

- to help children evaluate their work and recognize their own skills and progress. "Tell me what you and Nathan were doing when I took this photograph."

Analyzing Observation Notes and Portfolio Items

One brief observation note can help you learn about a child's social–emotional, physical, cognitive, and language development, as well as how he or she is learning literacy, math, science, and social studies concepts. Considered together, your observation notes, the child's portfolio, and the family information that you gather over time give you a portrait of a child's development and learning.

Let's consider what we can learn from the observation note about Tamika. Here it is again:

To assess a child's development and learning, you analyze your objective observation notes and the portfolio samples you collected with the curricular objectives in mind. Reflecting on the observation note above, you can see that you learned something about Tamika's social–emotional, physical, cognitive, and language development, as well as her literacy skills. You have information about the following objectives for development and learning:

3/18 – Circle time. T on my lap, singing "Thumbkin." T put up hands one at a time when I sang, "Here I am." Put hands behind back one at a time for "Run away." Said, "Run 'way." Walked away from circle after song. Came back. Said, "Sing."

Objective 1. Regulates own emotions and behaviors

Objective 2. Establishes and sustains positive relationships

Objective 3. Participates cooperatively and constructively in group situations

Objective 4. Demonstrates traveling skills

Objective 7. Demonstrates fine motor strength and coordination

Objective 8. Listens to and understands increasingly complex language

Objective 9. Uses spoken language to express thoughts and needs

To guide your planning, it is helpful to understand what children do when they are developing typically and the next steps that most children take. The information in chapter 1, "Knowing How Children Develop and Learn," and in chapter 3, "What Children Are Learning," can guide your thinking about what most children are able to do at each age and the next steps they usually take. This information will help you see that Tamika can do many things that are typical for children her age. She

- joins in singing familiar songs and fingerplays
- walks with her feet placed apart widely, holding her arms out for balance
- coordinates hand movements
- understands simple verbs, such as *run*
- makes simple requests, such as "Sing 'gain."
- supplies familiar language at the appropriate time when a favorite book is read aloud

These are some next steps that Tamika might take:

- begin to use words to identify feelings, for example, *happy* and *mad*
- begin to regulate her own behavior
- participate in activities with other children
- move in and out of play with other children
- handle objects with either hand
- carry objects while walking
- understand simple stories that are read aloud
- repeat phrases from predictable books
- understand many simple phrases used during daily routines and other familiar situations
- seek information from adults by gesturing or asking simple questions, such as "What's that?"

Using Information to Plan

Use what you know about Tamika to plan experiences that will promote her development and learning. Here are some things that you might do on the basis of what you know about Tamika and expect her to do next:

- Continue to sing simple songs and recite fingerplays with simple actions during morning circle time.

- Read books with simple, predictable language.

- Read books about feelings.

- Offer experiences that encourage Tamika to engage with Nathan and Jorge.

- Give Tamika simple tasks as she participates in daily routines. For example, ask, "Will you please put the basket of napkins on the table?"

- Answer Tamika's questions in order to encourage her to ask more.

- Provide pocketbooks and tote bags to encourage her to carry objects while walking.

Sharing Information With Families

Chapter 5 discusses conferences with families and the "Family Conference Form" that is included in the appendix of this book. The partial form on the next page shows how you might share information about Tamika's development and learning with her family.

Family Conference Form

Child's Name: __Tamika__   Date: __May 4, 2009__

Social–Emotional Development	Physical Development
Tamika joins our daily circle when we are singing, doing fingerplays, or reading simple books. Sometimes she walks away for a minute, but she usually comes back and joins the group again.	Tamika walks like a toddler. She places her feet apart widely and holds her arms out for balance. She can do simple fingerplays.
Oral Language Development and Literacy	**Cognitive Development**
Tamika makes simple requests, such as asking us to sing and to read books again. She shows that she understands a lot of verbs when she follows simple directions like "Lie down on your cot" or "Please get your coat." When we reread familiar stories, she is beginning to fill in the word if I omit one from a refrain.	Tamika names many common objects, such as ball, bottle, car, and dog. She responds to simple directions and requests. When she uses our toy phone she shows that she understands that a toy can stand for something else. Tamika shows her curiosity by gesturing and asking simple questions.

Mathematics, Science, Social Studies, and the Arts

Tamika is learning about math and science. She likes to fill boxes and buckets with toys, but she sometimes finds that they're too big. She puts a napkin on each plate when we set the table. She asks, "More?" when she wants more playdough or more food at lunch. She likes to help feed our fish.

Favorite Activities and Special Interests

Excellent family child care programs are based on two understandings: 1) how young children typically develop and learn and 2) how each child is developing and learning uniquely. These strategies will help you offer an excellent program:

Know and appreciate what makes each child special.

Collect and analyze information about each child's culture, family, strengths, and interests.

Offer routines and experiences that encourage children to develop new skills.

Talk with families about their children often.

Use what you learn about each child to plan and offer experiences that support his or her development and learning.

Observation is a powerful tool that will make you more successful in your work, so it will become part of your everyday care and teaching. Watching, listening, and thinking are important tools that help you guide children's progress.

Summary

As a family child care provider, you may have the pleasure of guiding a child's development and learning from the time he enters your program as a baby until he leaves your program as an older school-age child. You will watch and help him as he learns to walk, talk, read, solve problems, practice self-help skills, and regulate his own behavior. Yours is joyful and satisfying work!

This chapter focused on the many roles you play as a family child care provider. The secure relationships you develop with children give them a strong foundation for learning. You help them learn to get along with other children. You guide their behavior, support them as they learn through play, and guide their progress in all areas of development. The next chapter, "Building Partnerships With Families," focuses on another important role for family child care providers. It explains how to develop relationships with families, provide continuity between the child's home and your family child care home, and use a partnership approach to resolve differences.

General References

Bailey, B. (1997). *There's gotta be a better way: Discipline that works!* Oviedo, FL: Loving Guidance, Inc.

Bilmes, J. (2004). *Beyond behavior management: The six life skills children need to thrive in today's world.* St. Paul, MN: Redleaf Press.

Gartrell, D. (2004). *The power of guidance: Teaching social-emotional skills in early childhood classrooms.* Washington, DC: National Association for the Education of Young Children and Clifton Park, NY: Delmar Learning.

Jablon, J. R., Dombro, A. L., and Dichtelmiller, M. (2007). *The power of observation* (2nd ed.). Washington, DC: Teaching Strategies, Inc. and National Association for the Education of Young Children.

Kaiser, B., & Rasminsky, J. S. (1999). *Meeting the challenge: Effective strategies for challenging behaviours in early childhood environments.* Ottawa, Ontario: Canadian Child Care Federation.

McAfee, O., & Leong, D. J. (2007). *Assessing and guiding young children's development and learning* (4th ed.). Pearson Education, Inc.

McAfee, O., Leong, D. J., & Bodrova, E. (2004). *Basics of assessment: A primer for early childhood educators*. Washington, DC: National Association for the Education of Young Children.

Riley, D., San Juan, R. R., Klinkner, J., & Ramminger, A. (2008). *Social and emotional development: Connecting science and practice in early childhood settings*. St. Paul, MN: Redleaf Press.

5

Building Partnerships With Families

Building Partnerships With Families

Family child care providers are in a unique position to build strong, positive relationships with families. You have only a small number of families at any particular time, you see family members every day, and your relationship can continue for many years. This gives you a tremendous advantage because children benefit when their families and providers have positive relationships built with good communication, mutual respect, trust, and a commitment to providing the best care and education for the children.

In many ways, you are *sharing the care* with families. The issues you must discuss and agree upon with families are rooted in strong beliefs and ideas about practices. The partnership you create together is essential to the way children experience child care and how much they develop and learn during the years they spend with you.

This chapter explains the fifth component of *The Creative Curriculum for Family Child Care*. It offers practical ideas for working with families to develop partnerships based on trust and mutual respect. It has four sections:

Initial Contacts and Enrollment discusses the questions a family might ask; the information that families need from you; and the process of enrolling a child, including developing an individual care plan.

Getting to Know Families explores differences among families and the influence of culture upon child-rearing practices.

Communicating With Families shows how mutual trust is built through daily interactions with families, suggests some more formal ways of communicating, and explains how to conduct conferences with families.

Partnering for Children's Learning suggests a variety of ways families can participate in your program and describes resources that you can use to help them support children's learning at home.

Responding to Challenging Situations addresses ways to respond to families under stress and presents strategies for supporting the families of children with disabilities and the families of children who are dual-language learners. It also describes a partnership approach to resolving differences with families.

Initial Contacts and Enrollment

When a family first contacts you about child care, they often have number of concerns. These are the kinds of questions about which they are thinking:

Will my child…

- be safe and free from harm?
- receive a lot of attention?
- feel comfortable and happy in this child care home?
- receive warm, loving, and responsive care?
- still love me best?
- have interesting things to see and to do?
- learn to get along with other children?
- hear lots of language?
- be ready for school?

These questions reflect the uncertainties and fears that many families experience when they seek care for their children. Everything you do to assure families that your program will respond constructively to their concerns will encourage the trust and confidence essential to partnerships.

Determining Whether Your Program Is the Right Fit

Your program may or may not be the right one for a child and family. This is a decision that both you and the family will have to make. Families will have questions for you, and you will need information from each family. Together, you will determine whether your program is the right fit for everyone.

A family may call at any time to inquire about your program, but you do not want to take time away from the children to talk on the phone. Use an answering machine so you do not miss an important call if you are busy when it comes. Include a message about when you are available to talk and ask the caller to leave a phone number so that you can contact the family at another time.

When you speak with a family, take notes about important information such as the following:

- parent's(s') name(s), address, and phone numbers
- child's name and age
- hours of care required
- when care would begin

Families will need information from you as well. Be prepared to share the following information:

- your hours of operation
- the location of your family child care home
- your experience and qualifications
- the number and ages of the children in your program
- your fees
- names and phone numbers of references

If you and the family determine that enrollment is a good idea, set up a time for the family to visit when you will have time to talk. It is important for you to get to know one another and for you to meet the child. Some topics you might cover in this initial meeting with the family include the following:

- your philosophy and your use of a comprehensive curriculum to guide your planning for children of different ages
- your daily schedule and the kinds of experiences you offer children
- your approach to guiding children's behavior
- how you handle mealtimes, toilet training, and naps
- suggestions for easing hellos and good-byes

Use this initial contact with a family to determine whether your program is a good fit for the child. This may be the beginning of a long relationship. You need to feel comfortable with the family, and the family needs to feel comfortable with you. Pay attention to your own feelings and intuition before accepting a family.

Enrolling the Child and Family

Many providers have an enrollment form to gather basic information about each child and family. They record such information as the names of family members, the child's age, the names and ages of siblings, contact information, the child's health history, experiences with care away from home, and any special needs. Your licensing agency might provide registration forms for you to copy or adapt.

Family child care is a business. You should share clear, written policies and procedures with families so everyone knows what to expect. Provide information about the following:

- the hours during which you provide child care
- the meals and snacks you provide and what you expect families to contribute
- holidays and vacations when child care will not be provided
- your fees and payment schedule (including late fees)
- the need for written authorization if you are to give a child medicine
- your policy about what to do if their child is sick
- the names and ages of your own children who interact with the children attending your program, and the names of any other adults who may help care for the children

Information to be discussed and clarified with each family includes the following:

- the hours their child will attend and the need to notify you of any changes
- who will bring and pick up the child each day, including contact information and a list of individuals to whom you are authorized to release the child
- what you will do if a child gets sick, including which family member you will call first
- The name and phone number of the child's doctor or clinic (to consult in an emergency)
- any allergies the child may have and what should be done in the case of an allergic reaction

In addition to sharing basic information, signing an agreement about terms, and providing written policies, an informal conversation will enable you begin to learn more about each child and family. Here are some important open-ended questions to ask the family over time:

- What would you most like me to know about your child?
- How is your child comforted best?
- What does your child most enjoy doing?
- What does your child find particularly challenging or frustrating?
- What are your hopes and dreams for your child?
- What do you want your child to learn in my program?
- Are there any special traditions, celebrations, stories, or songs that are especially important to your family and your child?
- Are there any special concerns I should know about in order to care for your child well?

As you talk with each family, find out what language(s) the child hears and speaks at home. Ask which family member speaks which languages. Find out if the child knows any English. Especially if the child is a dual-language learner who is just beginning to learn English, ask the family to teach you some important words in their home language. Your use of them will help ease the child's entry into your program.

During these initial meetings, begin to share information about your daily schedule, routines, experiences, and other aspects of your curriculum. Remember that these initial meetings can take place over time. You do not have to ask all of these questions at once. You can continue to learn more about the family as you develop your partnership.

Developing an Individual Care Plan

When a child attends your program, you will be sharing the child's care with the family. The more you know about the child's daily routines and habits at home, the better you will be able to provide care that is consistent with the way the family cares for their child. The "Family and Child Information Form" enables you to obtain detailed information about how the child is cared for at home. For example, you might learn that an infant is a fitful sleeper who likes to be rocked to sleep, is startled by loud noises, and is soothed by singing. This information will be invaluable to you as you try to comfort the child. The form is included in the appendix of this volume. It includes questions about arrival and departure times, breast-feeding or bottle-feeding, food preferences and allergies, diapering needs, and sleeping habits. There are also questions about school-age children.

Once you have completed the form with the family, use the information to develop the child's individual care plan (ICP). As you can see in the example below, an ICP summarizes the information you obtained from a family about how best to care for their child. The plan is developed *with* the family when the child enters your program. A form for writing an ICP is also included in the appendix of this book.

Individual Care Plan

Child: Jeremy Soloman

Child's Date of Birth: 8-29-2008

Family Member(s): Karen Soloman

Date: 5-1-2009

Arrival	Eating
Mom will bring Jeremy at around 7:30 a.m.	Jeremy is nursing. Mom will bring expressed milk for him. She will usually breast-feed him at FCC before she leaves for work and again when she picks him up in the afternoon. He is eating infant cereal and strained vegetables and fruit. Mom thinks she will be adding more foods now and will coordinate with me. She also wants to start introducing a sippy cup and would like us to use one here as well.

Diapering	Dressing
Jeremy needs his diaper changed about 30–45 minutes after eating. He likes to be actively involved and enjoys playing with his fingers and toes during diapering.	Jeremy has a couple of extra sets of clothing in his cubby. Mom is not too worried if he spills something on his clothes. She does want him to have his shirt on when he goes outside in the summer and wants to make sure he wears a hat and mittens in the winter. She'll attach his mittens to his winter jacket so they don't get lost.

Sleeping	Departure
Jeremy takes two naps, one from 10:00–11:30 and another from 2:30–3:30. Mom likes to rock him gently in the rocking chair and sing a lullaby to help him sleep. She puts him in his crib just before he dozes off. He is a bit slow to wake up and needs a little time before he's ready to play.	Mom will pick Jeremy up at around 5:45. She'll call if she's going to be late, but she doesn't expect that to happen very often.

Developing an individual care plan with the child's family lets them know that you intend to share the care of their child. It also sends the message that you recognize families as experts on their children and that you want to benefit from their knowledge. Because young children develop and change so quickly, you will need to update the plan regularly.

After enrolling the child and developing a plan for the child's care, the next step is to ease the child into your program. Some children adjust easily and seem to fit right in. Others resist the transition and cling to their parents. Ask family members to try to arrange their schedules so they can stay for a while during the first few days to help their child feel comfortable and begin to trust you.

Getting to Know Families

Just as you get to know each child and use what you learn to build a relationship, you begin building partnerships with families by getting to know the most important people in each child's life. Learning about the unique characteristics, strengths, and issues important to each family will help you find ways to build the necessary trust and respect. Begin by recognizing the many ways families differ and how a family's culture shapes the way a child responds, interacts, and thinks.

Appreciating Differences

Every family is different. The traditional family—two parents and their children—is not as common as it once was. Many children are growing up with one parent. Some are being reared by grandparents or other relatives. Other children live with two mothers or two fathers. To appreciate differences among the families you serve, start by keeping an open mind about what constitutes a "family." Always remember that, to children, their families are the most important people in the world.

Each family brings a wide range of life experiences that shape who they are and how they relate to others. The level of education that family members have achieved, socioeconomic status, health issues, and length of time in this country also account for differences among families. Some are new parents and are very young, themselves. Others are caring for elderly or ill family members as well as their own children. Some are facing challenging circumstances such as unemployment; substance abuse; low literacy skills; unstable or unsafe housing; depression; or lack of access to a phone, computer, or transportation. Others are experiencing long separations from loved ones who are away for military service or in prison. You may have families who came to this country recently, who do not know the language well, and who are trying to understand how to fit in. They may expect to be here permanently or plan to return to their country of origin.

Most parents in your program will be working. Some may have demanding jobs with major responsibilities. Others may be working more than one job just to put food on the table and meet their family's basic needs. You may also have parents who are attending school or a training program. Parents may be struggling to balance the demands of work or school responsibilities with home responsibilities, finding little time for themselves or their child. Your sensitivity to these different life circumstances influences how families relate to you, and it can help you build the partnerships that are essential to providing high-quality care. Sometimes just being a responsive listener and reassuring families can go a long way.

Understanding the Influence of Culture

Culture involves the customary beliefs, values, and practices people learn from their families and communities, either through example (watching what others do) or through explicit instruction (being told what is expected). Culture affects how people communicate and interact with others, and it shapes their expectations of how others will respond. Because every culture has its own set of rules and expectations, different cultures interpret what people do and say differently. Culture has a very strong influence on child-rearing practices, beliefs, and goals.

It is common to associate "culture" with ethnic and religious groups. In fact, there are many different cultural groups. Families who are in the military, for example, have a distinct culture. Because they move around so much, their friends in the military become their extended families and provide support to one another when spouses are deployed. The fact that a family member is far away and often in danger has an influence on child-rearing practices and family relationships. Another example is the culture shared by people who are deaf. Many use a common language, American Sign Language, as their primary way of communicating with one another. In the hearing community, it is sometimes considered socially unacceptable for people to stare intently at one another. In the deaf community, watching each other closely is critical to communication.

Try to learn as much as possible about the cultures of the families in your program, keeping in mind that every family is different. Try not to generalize about any group's characteristics. Consider the many factors that influence the practices and values of an individual family, including the family's country of origin, its social class there and here, the parents' educational background, and whether extended family members live in the home. Rather than making assumptions about cultural influences, it is better to keep an open mind and consider the values behind each family's beliefs and practices. For example, in some families only men speak about matters that relate to the family. In others, it is not polite to make direct eye contact, which might make is difficult for you to assess how well you are communicating. You have to be comfortable with the idea that you may have different relationships with different families and that you might communicate a little differently with each. Nevertheless, all of your relationships can be equally positive.

Listed below are a variety of questions to help you learn more about each family. Use your judgment about what questions to ask of each family and when. Keep in mind that not all families are comfortable with responding to direct questions. You can learn a lot by observing how family members interact with their child. Be selective about the kinds of questions you ask each family.

- Who are the people in the child's immediate family?
- Who are the decision makers in the family? Are decisions made by one person or several people?
- Do all family members live in the same household?
- How often has the family moved?
- Who is the primary caregiver for the family's young children?
- How are children's names chosen?
- How does the family balance children's independence with doing things for them?
- When should toilet learning begin, and how should it be handled?
- What, when, and how are children fed?
- How is discipline handled?
- Do family members have different and distinct roles in rearing children?
- Are boys and girls treated differently?
- Is it acceptable for children to be noisy and to get dirty?
- How do adults respond to children's questions?
- How do people interact with one another? Do they look each other in the eye? Are they taught to pause and think carefully about a response before giving it? Do they touch each other as they communicate?
- How do families show respect for elders? For children?

Communicating With Families

Partnerships depend upon ongoing and open communication. Families want to know all the details about their children's experiences during the day, everything from what and how much they ate to what and with whom they played and how they reacted to events. You need important information from families as well. Because you see families every day, you have many opportunities to exchange information. Several times during the year, you might also want to have family conferences.

Making the Most of Daily Exchanges

Daily exchanges are the primary way to communicate with family members and keep everyone informed about what is happening at home and at the program. Respectful and sincere interactions show children that the most important people in their lives—their families and you—are connected and like each other.

Here are some suggestions for daily exchanges with families:

Greet each child and family personally. Use their names. Observe indications of how they are feeling and say something specific about the child, the family, or your plans for the day.

Share information about something the child has accomplished or about an event that involves the child. News can be shared in the morning, but the end of the day is often a good time to talk with families about what their child has done and to explain its significance. You might say, "Rosa worked very hard to finish a new puzzle today. Let me show it to you. She didn't give up until she figured it out. Her ability to stay with a task until it's finished is important to her learning."

Solicit their insights and advice about their child. You might prompt, "I see that Nathan doesn't want to say good-bye to you today. Can you think of any particular reason?"

Give support to families when needed. For example, you might respond, "Thank you for letting me know about his grandmother's illness. I'll give him extra attention today, and we'll talk about her."

Be a good listener. Active listening skills convey that parents' concerns and ideas are taken seriously. You might tell a parent, "I understand how upset you are about the biting incident. I can assure you that I am taking steps to prevent more biting."

Make sure you understand what is being said. If there is uncertainty about a family member's statement, clarify your understanding: "Tell me whether I understand what you are saying. I think I heard you say…"

In communicating with families, try to be specific and factual. Vague or subjective comments can leave family members uncertain about what you mean or make them defensive. Notice the difference between the subjective and objective comments in the two examples below. Think about how the parent might feel in each case.

Subjective Comments	The Parent's Thoughts
When Jeremy's mother comes to get him at the end of the day, you tell her, "Jeremy was very crabby today! I had the hardest time trying to comfort him."	"What did he do? How did you try to comfort him? Why didn't you call me? He's not crabby at home. I'm not sure you know how to take care of my baby. Maybe something is wrong with him or with me as a parent."

Objective Comments	The Parent's Thoughts
At nap time, you call Jeremy's mother to discuss his fussiness. You tell her, "Jeremy cried when he drank his bottle this morning. I tried holding him the way you showed me, but it didn't help. Do you have any suggestions for me?"	"I wonder what's wrong. I appreciate being asked for my advice and ideas. I know his family child care provider is doing all she can to take care of him."
When Jeremy's mother arrives at the end of the day, you tell her, "Jeremy was still a bit fussy when he ate this afternoon. He was pulling on his ear, so I wonder if he has an infection. Maybe he is still just adjusting to me, though. What do you think?"	"Perhaps he is not used to being in family child care yet, but maybe he is getting sick. If this continues, I'll take him to the clinic for a checkup. I feel good about leaving Jeremy with this provider. I know she will call me if she has any concerns."

Subjective Comments	Parent's Thoughts
When Nathan's father comes to pick him up at the end of the day, you tell him, "Nathan was such a good boy today. He just makes my day."	"I wonder what he did. Nathan is a real challenge at home. He won't clean up his room or cooperate when we ask him to do things. If he is good here but challenging at home, are we doing something wrong?"

Objective comments	Parent's Thoughts
When Nathan's father comes to pick him up, you tell him, "Today, Nathan really helped me. While I was putting lunch on the table, Nathan sat with Tamika and Jorge and showed them the pictures in his favorite book. Then he went with them to wash hands."	"My son is able to cooperate and relate well to other children. I guess the bedtime stories we read to him every night have made a difference, even if I have to read the same stories over and over! I feel good about the way he is developing and learning."

The examples above show how being specific and factual in your daily communications with families gives them helpful information. Families know that you are really taking an interest in their children and that you genuinely care about their well-being. In addition to informal oral exchanges, there are brief written forms of communication. Here are a few ideas:

Daily communication form—Create a form with space for families to record information about their

child when they arrive at the program each day. Request information that is basic to the child's daily care and explain that it helps you meet each child's current needs more effectively. You may need to encourage parents to take the time to complete this form when they bring their child. Request any information that you find helpful, such as when the child last ate, when her diaper was last changed, her general mood that day, how well she slept last night, when she will be picked up, and who will be picking her up.

A family resource area—If you have space in a corner or on a wall to display parent resources or announcements, that is an efficient way to share information with families.

Electronic mail—Sending e-mail is a quick way to stay in touch and to share specific information. Find out from families if they would like to communicate in this way.

A Web site—Many center-based programs have a Web site where program news is posted as well as articles of interest and photos of classroom events. Why not create a Web site for your program? You may have a family member who can help you set one up and even assist in keeping it up-to-date. An older school-age child might be learning to do this in school.

Journals—A simple journal for each family is a place for each of you to write entries and share information. The journal can travel with the child and family from their home to yours and back.

Holding Conferences With Families

A formal conference with each family should be held at least twice a year and more often if needed. Conferences are a time to sit together, uninterrupted, and talk as partners about caring for their child. They are opportunities to share information, observations, and questions. You can solve problems together when necessary and celebrate new milestones and accomplishments. If a child has a diagnosed disability, you can express your interest in participating in the meetings of the team of people who develop goals for the Individualized Family Service Plan (for a child under age three) or the Individualized Education Program (for children age 3 and older). Preparation and the many positive interactions you have already had with the family help ensure a successful conference.

Here are steps to take as you prepare for a family conference:

- Arrange a time that is convenient for you and the family and find out whom they would like to include in the conference.

- Let the family know what to expect. When you set up the conference, explain that conferences are a time to focus entirely on their child.

- Find out what the family is interested in learning about and whether there are any special issues they want to discuss.

- Review your observation notes and samples of the child's work that you want to share. This will help the family understand more about their child's experiences and accomplishments at the program.

- Be prepared to share what the child is learning. The information in chapter 3, "What Children Are Learning," will help you explain the significance of what each child is able to do.

- If language differences might be a barrier, arrange for someone to interpret. Many families know someone who can serve as an interpreter. If a family does not, try to make other arrangements. (It is not usually a good idea to ask a child to interpret.)

Start the conference by sharing your observation of something new, interesting, or delightful that their child has done or said. Invite family members to share what they have noticed about their child's development and learning and what their child talks about.

In the appendix, you will find a "Family Conference Form" to use as a record of the conference. Under the appropriate heading on the form, highlight the child's new discoveries and skills. Offer specific examples from your observation notes.

Throughout your discussion, encourage families to share their observations, questions, challenges, and joys. Explain that this is time to exchange information and that combining what each of you knows will give all of you the clearest possible understanding of their child. In addition to recording your own ideas, ask families for their ideas when you discuss the other sections of the form: "Favorite Activities and Special Interests" and "Family Comments and Special Circumstances." Family conferences are also good times to update the "Individual Care Plan" form you complete for each child.

Talk about each other's expectations for the child's development and learning. Together, complete the "Next Steps at Family Child Care and at Home" section of the "Family Conference Form." This will become your blueprint for working with the child. Keep it where you will have ready access to it, so you can remind yourself of areas you want to focus on during the next few months. At the next conference, the form can serve as a starting point for your discussion.

Partnering for Children's Learning

Families have been teaching their children since birth, so they are already your partners in supporting their children's learning. By inviting them to participate in your program and by sharing resources, you can gain valuable support and strengthen their confidence in their parenting skills.

Inviting Families to Participate

When you invite families to visit and to participate in the program as much as possible, you send a very positive message that you view the relationship as a real partnership. An open-door policy says that you are confident about your program and the way you care for their children. You want families to know that they are always welcome and that their involvement—no matter how extensive or limited—enhances the program and their children's experience.

Almost every family has something to offer your program and can make a meaningful contribution. The more possibilities they are offered, the more likely you are to involve every family. Here are some possible ways by which families can participate:

- gathering materials, such as old magazines, fabric scraps, collections (for example, bottle caps, buttons, keys, or shells), dress-up clothes, and toys

- helping with special projects, such as building a sandbox, making doll clothes, or constructing an easel

- participating in celebrations, such as birthday or holiday parties or celebrating children's learning at the end of a study

- accompanying you and the children on a field trip

- joining you and the children for a meal

- helping with an activity such as cooking, reading to children, or putting together a photo album

- sharing a special skill with the children

Keep in mind that parents are not the only family members who might want to participate in your program. Grandparents, for example, might have more free time to share than parents and may have a great deal of patience with young children. They might enjoy an opportunity to feed an infant, read to a child, play games and sing with the children, help a child settle for a nap, teach preschool and school-age children a skill such as knitting, or help with a woodworking project. Make a special effort to include a father or another significant male who is a steady influence in the child's life: the mother's partner or husband, an uncle, an older sibling, a grandfather, another relative, or a family friend. Find out which adults are important in a child's life. Learn about their interests, jobs, hobbies, and what they would like to share with the children. They may be able to make a positive contribution that will benefit everyone.

Supporting Children's Learning at Home

Children are learning all the time, when they are with you and when they are with their families. As a professional family child care provider who has taken the time to learn and use a comprehensive curriculum to guide your program planning, you have knowledge and experience in supporting children's positive development and learning. Sharing aspects of your curriculum and other resources with families can be a very effective way to ensure that children are getting the best preparation for success in school and in life. *The Creative Curriculum for Family Child Care* includes two resources for sharing ideas. They are 1) the letters to families about routines and experiences and 2) the set of selected *LearningGames.*

Letters to families—At the end of each of chapters 6–20, you will find a letter to families. Each sample letter explains why a particular routine or experience is an important part of your program, how you support children's learning and development in your family child care program, and how you hope to work together with families. You may adapt the letters or use them as they are. Sharing them periodically during the year or at a family conference will help families understand what you are doing every day to help children learn through routines and meaningful play experiences. The letters are also included on the CD-ROM, so you can print them easily if you have the necessary equipment.

LearningGames—The 68 *LearningGames* activities that are part of this curriculum are a resource to use and share with individual families at appropriate times. The ideas in most of these games will already be familiar to you, and, if you use them in your child care home, parents will receive the message that these are important interactions that professionals and *families* can have with children. Each activity helps teach families how everyday interactions and simple games support their children's positive relationships and important learning. Several games are listed at the end of each of the 4 chapters on routines and the 11 chapters on experiences. Games are included for each age-group from birth to age 5, along with suggestions for sharing them with families. These games involve interactions that you have with the children in your care, so families will see you demonstrating them. Each game also lists a children's book that is related to the game. The appendix of volume 2 includes a list of the games and the curricular objectives that each game addresses.

Made of sturdy material, the one-page game instructions may be lent to families and then returned to you. It would be a good idea to set up a system to keep track of each game you lend to a family and when it is returned. As you become familiar with the games and learn more about the children and families, you can select the game that is right for the child and of interest to his or her family at a particular time.

You may find that families react differently to the *LearningGames.* Some may love the idea of posting a game on their refrigerator for a week or two and learning something new to do with their child. Others may be less interested, although these families may change their minds when they see you using these simple, research-validated games in your program; see how interested their children are in playing the games; and notice other families' enthusiasm for the games. Be sensitive to each family's needs and interests. Base your selection of *LearningGames* for each family on your knowledge of their child's strengths, needs, and interests.

Responding to Challenging Situations

Despite all of the positive steps you take to build a partnership with each family, you will encounter challenging situations. Some families are struggling with meeting basic needs, and the ongoing stress makes it difficult for them to be available to their children. You may have children who are learning more than one language and children with disabilities. These families need your understanding and support. Even in the best relationships, misunderstandings and conflicts emerge. Challenging situations must be handled carefully and positively in order to maintain a partnership with every family.

Supporting Families Who Are Under Stress

Families experience different kinds of stress, and they may have difficulty coping. Ongoing and unrelenting stress can come from many sources:

- living in a violent community
- limited financial resources
- seeking employment or job training without knowing whether they will be able to continue bringing their child to the program
- long commutes to a job
- limited transportation
- a job that does not allow flexibility in work hours to accommodate family needs
- a family member with a physical disability, physical or mental illness, cognitive delays, or low literacy skills
- domestic and/or substance abuse
- adapting to a new culture and/or language
- substandard, overcrowded housing or living in a shelter
- barriers to health care

Parents who are under stress from these or other life situations do not always have the emotional energy or physical resources to nurture their children. Sometimes they have trouble meeting their children's most basic needs. They may not be able to solve problems, communicate positively with their children, or give them the attention and affirmation they need. Their discipline may be inconsistent, overly punitive, or nonexistent. For many children in these circumstances, life is unpredictable and dangerous. They may seem angry, withdrawn, or fearful when they come to your program.

The stress a family is experiencing can affect the way they relate to you. Because you see families every day and get to know them well, you will probably be able to recognize when a family is under stress. In many cases, because they trust you, they may tell you about problems they are having. Try to be as supportive as you can. Avoid adding to the stress by being overly critical, such as when a parent forgets to bring boots for her child despite several reminders. Also be mindful of parental stress when you need to discuss a problem you are having with a child. Sometimes it is wise to wait for a better time. Seek ways to reassure families about the positive things they are doing.

Most communities have social and legal service agencies that offer resources and guidance to families in need. Find out what exists in your area. Perhaps you can put together some information for families to share as needed. This might include

- an up-to-date list of community agencies and hotlines for referrals
- brochures and resources for families to borrow
- a list of support groups that deal with family issues

Parenting is one of the most important jobs in the world, yet there is very little training for this critical role. Parents who were fortunate enough to have caring, nurturing experiences when they were children have a solid foundation for becoming supportive parents, themselves. Those who had less constructive experiences still want the best for their children and are doing what they think is right. Although some parents do things that bother you, hold to the belief that most are doing the best they can. Learn as much as you can about the strengths and needs of each family so that you have realistic expectations and can individualize your approach to your partnership. Your way of working with one family will not necessarily be the same as with another.

Supporting the Families of Children With Disabilities

It is very possible that you will have children in your program who have special needs. Many of these children and families will already be receiving early intervention services for a developmental delay. Other children may have special needs that have not yet been identified. Sometimes a family child care provider is the first to detect that a child is not developing typically and that there may be a problem. You may be able to help the family find specialists to determine whether there is a particular problem and to obtain the necessary services.

When parents first learn that their child is not developing typically, they often experience a mix of emotions that is unique to dealing with this new reality. Knowing the emotional stages experienced by many families of children with disabilities will help you offer appropriate support.[1]

1. **Denial**—Initially parents may deny the child's special needs or disability. Recognize that this is a first step in coming to terms with their child's disability and do not put any pressure on the family to accept what may be obvious to others.

2. **Projection of blame**—A common reaction to learning that their child is not perfect is for families to want to blame someone else. There may or may not be any basis for the accusations same families make. You might hear family members say things such as, "If only they would have…." You may even become a target of blame. Patience and a willingness to listen without taking sides will help you and the family through this stage.

3. **Fear**—At this stage, the family is still learning about the special needs of their child. The information is probably new to them, and they may question it. You or someone in your program can offer support by helping them sort through the information and by learning about the disability, yourself.

4. **Guilt**—Some families worry that they did not do all they could have to prevent the disability. Their thinking might or might not be rational. Remember that this is a difficult time for the family. At this stage, the family may find it helpful if you offer ideas about channeling their energy into activities to support their child.

5. **Mourning or grief**—The reality of a disability often brings tremendous grief, pain, and disappointment. Families must work through many emotions before being able to accept their child's disability. You can help simply by listening and showing that you care.

6. **Withdrawal**—Withdrawing in order to manage their powerful emotions is often a healthy and essential step for families. You may become concerned about family members as you see them withdraw and become isolated. Continue to try to communicate with them, and offer your understanding and respect for what they are experiencing.

7. **Rejection**—At this stage, the family member may actually show some signs of rejecting their child's disability. This can mean failing to recognize the child's capabilities and strengths or setting unrealistic goals for the child. Your observations of the child and examples of what the child *can* do will help families realize their child's strengths and capabilities and help them set realistic goals for the child.

8. **Acceptance**—At this stage, the parent is able to accept the child with his or her disability and offer the support that helps the child develop and learn.

Keep in mind that there is no set timetable for how quickly or slowly family members progress through these stages. Not all families go through each stage, and family members sometimes cycle through the stages more than once. An event, such as seeing another child who is developing at a typical pace, can trigger feelings all over again. It may be painful for you to observe families while they are experiencing the powerful emotions involved during these stages.

You also have to be realistic and recognize the limits of your own time, energy, knowledge, and skills. You can encourage family members to seek additional support from specialists who are more familiar with their child's disability than you are. You should ask to be included in the team that will come together to develop a plan for supporting the child's full inclusion in your program.

Supporting the Families of Children Who Are Dual-Language Learners

Dual-language learners comprise nearly 25 percent of the school-age population in the United States today. As explained in chapter 1, a dual-language learner is a child who is learning more than one language. The child and family both need your understanding and support.

Families of dual-language learners have a variety of expectations. Some want their children to learn English as quickly as possible. Others have concerns about their children's losing the ability to communicate in their home language. Families may think that they have to choose between their home languages and English. Fortunately, this is not the case. Maintaining and developing children's home languages actually helps them acquire English. Children who have larger vocabularies and language skills in their home languages are able to learn English more quickly because language skills in their home languages are the foundation for learning another language.

As a family child care provider, you play an important role in supporting families to encourage their children's optimal language development. Reassure families that children can learn English without losing their home languages. Here are some ways you can support the families of children who are dual-language learners:

Encourage families to continue to speak their home languages with their children. Help families understand how important it is to talk, sing, and play with their children in their home languages. Suggest resources, such as the local library where they can check out books in their home languages to read to their child. If family members do not have strong reading skills, encourage them to "talk" the books by discussing the pictures with their child and making up their own stories. Many cultures have strong oral storytelling traditions. Encourage parents to share stories with their children about their countries of origin and their own childhoods.

Children benefit by maintaining their home languages while learning English. One of the most important benefits is the ability to communicate with family members who do not speak English. Language is a vital part of culture and family history. If children lose the ability to communicate in their home language, they may also lose the ability to communicate with older family members and other members of their cultural group. Giving children the gift of being bilingual is one that will benefit them throughout their lives.

Bring the families' languages into your home. Play songs in children's home languages. Invite families to record songs, read books, and tell stories on audiocassettes that can be played during the day in your program. Children will not only hear their home languages, but they will also hear the familiar voices of their family members. That may comfort them and ease their transition into your program.

Share information about dual-language learning. Let families know that most children who are learning English after already having a foundation in their home languages go through a nonverbal stage in which they do not speak in either language. During this period, the children still communicate with gestures, vocalizations, and body language. This is very typical, so there is no reason to be concerned. Continuing to offer the child many opportunities to hear, use, and play with both languages is the best way to support children during this nonverbal stage.

Communicate with families in their preferred languages when possible. When communicating with families who speak a home language other than English, find out their preferred language for communicating with you. Provide written communications in the family's preferred language to help them understand program news and events and catch details they may have missed in face-to-face exchanges.

If you and a family do not share a common language, arrange for the services of an interpreter for family meetings and conferences. It is best to avoid asking a child to interpret. Some parents do not consider that to be a child's responsibility. Furthermore, you and the family might use language that the child is not able to interpret accurately. You might also want to discuss concerns about which you do not want the child to become anxious. A bilingual parent from another family might be willing to interpret, but be sure to follow confidentiality guidelines. Another great source for interpreters could be local community centers, churches, and social service agencies that work with families from diverse language backgrounds.

Help families understand what you are saying when you speak with them in English. When you do speak English with families, a few simple strategies can help you communicate your message. Use pictures, objects, gestures, and other body language to provide context and visual cues. Speak slowly and clearly. Be careful to avoid idiomatic phrases with meanings that may be hard for families to understand, such as "He slept like a log" or "You're pulling my leg." Pause and give families plenty of time to respond. Many adults who are learning a new language need time to interpret information they hear in the new language into the home language, formulate a response, and then interpret it from the home language back into the new language. This process requires patience.

Support families as their child transitions to school. Enrolling a child school can be problematic, especially for families who do not understand and speak much English. Families may need assistance with filling out forms, understanding school requirements, and communicating with school personnel. Help connect families with resources that can support them in this transition. Let families know that all children, regardless of language background or immigration status, are entitled to attend public school and receive some form of language support services.

Resolving Differences: A Partnership Approach

If you work with families who share your values and beliefs and have similar life experiences and personal characteristics, you are more likely to interpret what they say and do in similar ways. If you work with families who are very different from you—and if you know little about their beliefs and practices—miscommunication and misunderstandings can easily take place. Understanding and respecting practices that are different from your own help you to build positive relationships with all families.

When the adults in their lives share a consistent approach, children are more likely to feel safe and secure in your program. This does not mean that you have to agree about everything. There will probably be times when you and a family will have different points of view about caring for their child. Always ask yourself this question: How can we work out our differences in a positive way?

Here are examples of how misunderstandings can occur because your views about a situation differ from that of a family member. Following each example, a resolution that respects the partnership is suggested.

Situation	Your View	The Family's View
After careful observations over time, you are concerned that a toddler's language is delayed. You suggest an evaluation by a speech specialist. The parents fail to make an appointment with a specialist.	If a problem exists, it should be identified as early as possible. Parents should want to get all the help they can get for their child.	My child is fine. There's nothing wrong.

Partnership View: There may be a number of reasons why parents might resist having their child evaluated by a specialist for a possible problem. It is not unusual for parents to be reluctant to accept that there is a problem the first time you talk about it. (See the section of this chapter on "Supporting the Families of Children With Disabilities.") If you suspect that this is the reason for their not following your advice, be patient for a while. Suggest that you all observe more carefully for a few weeks and keep in touch about what you learn. Try to find out about community resources the family could consult and provide that information to them.

Situation	Your View	The Family's View
A family requests that you continue their practice of toileting their 12-month-old child. They explain how they are aware of when their child is about to urinate or defecate, and they simply take him to the toilet in time.	"Catching" a child in time to bring him to the potty is not toilet learning. Children let us know when they have the muscle control and awareness to use the toilet. That is the most appropriate time to begin the process of toilet learning.	It is important for us to train our children to use the toilet at this age. We did it with our other children, and it works just fine. It saves the cost of disposable diapers and is better for the environment.

Partnership View: Toilet learning is a topic that you and families are likely to have strong feelings about and perhaps different approaches. It is helpful to discuss the family's approach to toilet learning when they are first considering enrolling their child in your program. You should also explain the steps that you typically use when helping children learn to use the toilet. This may prevent some problems. When toileting practices differ, it is important to listen to the family's perspective and find some aspect of their approach to affirm. You can explain, "As you can imagine, it's more challenging with a group of children. I will do my best to watch for the signs you mentioned and take him to the potty." This approach conveys your appreciation of the family's preference without making a commitment that you cannot fulfill.

Situation	Your View	The Family's View
When you first meet a toddler's grandfather, he tells you that he does not understand why you do not spank his grandson for hitting other children.	You teach children to be gentle with others by modeling gentleness and guiding their behavior in positive ways. You stop children when they hit others and help them learn to verbalize their thoughts and feelings instead of hitting.	The grandfather believes in using a strong-handed approach to rearing children. His philosophy is "Spare the rod, spoil the child." It worked for him with his children. He's concerned about his grandson's "bad" behavior.

Partnership View: When a family member whom you do not know well comes to discuss a concern, it is helpful to begin by first taking a few minutes to get to know the person better before attempting to address the issue. Explain that you understand the family's concerns. You might tell this grandfather, "It sounds as though it's very important to you that your grandson learn how to get along with others. Is that right?" Then take the time to discuss your program's approach to promoting positive behavior. Share the social–emotional objectives of the curriculum and talk about how you help children develop self-regulation skills and other positive behaviors.

Summary

When you develop partnerships with children's families, everyone benefits. Children feel more secure and comfortable when their families and child care provider share their knowledge respectfully and interact positively. They are more likely to experience consistency in the care they receive when families are invited to share what they want for and know about their children. Families feel more secure about leaving their children in the care of someone who takes the time to build relationships with them. They gain confidence in their parenting skills when you invite families to participate in the program and when you share resources that support their children's learning at home. You acquire valuable support and information from families that enable you to get to know each child better and provide more individualized care. Your partnerships enable children to relate positively with others, control their behavior, and have the skills and motivation to learn.

---

[1] From *Parents as Partners in Education: Families and Schools Working Together* (6th ed.), by E. H. Berger, 2004, Upper Saddle River, NJ: Pearson Education. Copyright 2004 by Pearson Education. Adapted with permission.

Appendix

Objectives for Development and Learning: Birth to Age 6

Social–Emotional

1. Regulates own emotions and behaviors

a. Manages feelings

b. Follows limits and expectations

2. Establishes and sustains positive relationships

a. Forms relationships with adults

b. Interacts with peers

c. Makes friends

d. Responds to emotional cues

3. Participates cooperatively and constructively in group situations

a. Participates in classroom activities

b. Balances needs and rights of self and others

c. Solves social problems

Physical

4. Demonstrates traveling skills

a. Walks

b. Runs

c. Gallops and skips

5. Demonstrates balancing skills

a. Sits and stands

b. Walks on beam

c. Jumps and hops

6. Demonstrates gross motor manipulative skills

a. Throws

b. Catches

c. Kicks

7. Demonstrates fine motor strength and coordination

a. Uses fingers and hands

b. Uses writing tools

c. Uses scissor tools

Oral Language

8. Listens to and understands increasingly complex language

a. Comprehends oral language

b. Follows oral directions

9. Uses spoken language to express thoughts and needs

a. Tells about another time or place

b. Speaks clearly

c. Uses conventional grammar

d. Uses an expanding expressive vocabulary

10. Uses appropriate conversational and other communication skills

a. Engages in conversations

b. Uses social rules of language

Cognitive

11. Demonstrates positive approaches to learning

a. Attends and engages

b. Persists

c. Solves problems

d. Shows curiosity and motivation

e. Shows flexibility and inventiveness

12. Remembers and connects experiences

a. Recognizes and recalls

b. Makes connections

13. Classifies and sorts

a. Classifies

b. Sorts

14. Uses symbols and images to represent something not present

a. Thinks symbolically

b. Engages in sociodramatic play

Literacy

15. **Demonstrates phonological awareness**

   a. Attends to rhyme

   b. Attends to alliteration

   c. Attends to smaller and smaller units of sound

16. **Demonstrates knowledge of the alphabet**

   a. Identifies and names letters

   b. Uses letter–sound knowledge

17. **Demonstrates knowledge of print and its uses**

   a. Uses and appreciates books

   b. Uses print concepts

18. **Comprehends and responds to books and other texts**

   a. Interacts during read-alouds and book conversations

   b. Uses emergent storybook-reading skills

   c. Retells stories

19. **Demonstrates emergent writing skills**

   a. Writes name

   b. Writes to convey meaning

Mathematics

20. **Uses number concepts and operations**

   a. Counts

   b. Quantifies

   c. Connects numerals with their quantities

21. **Explores and describes spatial relationships and shapes**

   a. Understands spatial relationships

   b. Understands shapes

22. **Compares and measures**

23. **Demonstrates knowledge of patterns**

Science and Technology

24. **Uses scientific inquiry skills**

25. **Demonstrates knowledge of the characteristics of living things**

26. **Demonstrates knowledge of the physical properties of objects and materials**

27. **Demonstrates knowledge of the Earth's environment**

28. **Uses tools and other technology to perform tasks**

Social Studies

29. **Demonstrates knowledge about self**

30. **Shows basic understanding of people and how they live**

31. **Explores change related to familiar people or places**

32. **Demonstrates simple geographic knowledge**

The Arts

33. **Explores the visual arts**

34. **Explores musical concepts and expression**

35. **Explores dance and movement concepts**

36. **Explores drama through actions and words**

English Language Acquisition

37. **Demonstrates progress in listening to and understanding English**

38. **Demonstrates progress in speaking English**

Child Planning Form

Week of: _____

Child:	**Child:**
Current information:	Current information:
Plans:	Plans:
Child:	**Child:**
Current information:	Current information:
Plans:	Plans:

TeachingStrategies™
CURRICULUM

Group Planning Form

Week of: _____

Changes to the Environment:

Changes to Routines and Schedule:

Family Involvement:

Group Planning Form, continued

Week of: _____

Events and Play Experiences

	Monday	Tuesday	Wednesday	Thursday	Friday
Morning meeting					
Choice time					
Outdoor time					
Read-aloud time					
Special activities					

Ideas for next week:

TeachingStrategies™
CURRICULUM

Family Conference Form

Child's Name: _____   Date: _____

Social–Emotional Development	Physical Development

Oral Language Development and Literacy	Cognitive Development

Mathematics, Science, Social Studies, and the Arts

Favorite Activities and Special Interests

Family Comments and Special Circumstances

Next Steps at Family Child Care and at Home

FCC Provider's Signature: _____   Date: _____

Family Signature(s): _____   Date: _____

Family & Child Information Form

Child:	
Child's Date of Birth:	
Family Member(s):	
Date:	

About Your Family

Tell me about your family.

What language(s) do you speak at home?

What are some activities your family enjoys doing together?

Is this your child's first early childhood program experience?

What is the best way for our program to exchange information with you about your child?

Favorite Activities and Special Interests

What are some of your child's favorite activities?

With whom does your child play? How do they play together? What do they play together?

What is your child most interested in right now? How can you tell?

Does your child have favorite toys? How does your child play with them?

What books does your child like to read? Does your child read alone or with you?

What songs does your child know and like to sing?

Family & Child Information, continued

School

If your child is in school, please answer the following questions:

In what grade is your child?

What is the name of your child's teacher?

What are your child's favorite subjects?

Will your child have homework? If so, do you want your child to do homework at my family child care home or at your home?

If homework should be done at FCC, how should I help?

Does your child prefer to do homework right away, or to relax or do other activities first?

Arrival/Departure

What time will you usually arrive?

What will help you and your child say good-bye to each other in the morning?

What time will you usually come to pick up your child?

What will help you and your child say hello to each other at the end of the day?

Family & Child Information, continued

Mealtime

Describe your child's mealtimes and how your child eats or is fed.

What are some of your child's favorite foods? What foods does your child dislike?

Is your child sensitive or allergic to any foods? If so, what are they?

Are there any foods that you don't want your child to eat?

Nap Time/Resting

Does your child nap during the day? If so, what helps your child fall asleep?

How long does your child usually sleep?

When does your child usually sleep?

If your child does not nap during the day, does your child have a rest time? What activities does your child usually do during this rest time?

Family & Child Information, continued

Other Routines

Does your child use the toilet? If so, are there any special instructions for toileting? How does your child let you know that he or she needs to use the toilet?

If not, how often do you change your child's diaper? When does your child usually need a diaper change?

Is there anything special that we should know about dressing and undressing your child?

How much help does your child need with toothbrushing?

Additional Information

What else would you like us to know about your child and family?

Individual Care Plan

Child: _____

Child's Date of Birth: _____

Family Member(s): _____

Date: _____

Arrival	Eating

Diapering	Dressing

Sleeping	Departure

Index